JANIE HYDRICK, EDITOR
NANCY WILDERMUTH, CONTRIBUTING EDITOR

Whole Language

EMPOWERMENT AT THE
CHALK FACE

THE PROCEEDINGS OF THE 1989
NATIONAL COUNCIL OF TEACHERS OF ENGLISH
DAY OF WHOLE LANGUAGE

NEW YORK • TORONTO • LONDON • AUCKLAND • SYDNEY

Cover design by Vincent Ceci.
Cover illustration by Sara Gilles.
Design by Marjory Dressler.

12 11 10 9 8 7 6 5 4 3 2 1   1 2 3 4 5/9

ISBN 0-590-49087-7

Printed in the U.S.A.

Dedicated to all teachers and
learners who have helped me see
myself as both.

J.H.

CONTENTS

Janie Hydrick, Conference Chairperson

Preface

The title of this book comes from Ken Goodman's chapter. He refers to the British term for the place where curriculum happens. "Their metaphor, when they want to talk about the real world, is the coal face, where the miner is down in the coal mine facing that coal seam." In classrooms where curriculum is brought in from other sources in response to presumed needs or arbitrary requirements, confrontation in the trenches is an appropriate metaphor. But empowerment at the chalk face is just a beginning point for empowerment in all aspects of life and learning.

I invite you to read each chapter in this book. Some you may agree with wholly. Others may make you wonder, question, even disagree wholly. I hope you experience some of each. Yetta Goodman writes in her chapter, "My developing beliefs about whole language are honed by my interactions with teachers who share with me what they are doing and who challenge what I'm saying. We will never agree on all aspects of whole language, but it will be through shared understandings about the nature of our agreements and disagreements that whole language will be nurtured."

How can we connect and make sense of what we hear, see, feel, and think about whole language? I invite each of you to build a framework for yourselves as you read this book. The framework will come from looking at, using, and growing with whole language. It will not be a framework in the sense of a permanent structure to be filled in with wood, cement, and stone, but a framework much like a garden trellis: an open structure for guiding and supporting life and growth, a dynamic framework with the old always giving seed and nourishment for the new—and, to continue the metaphor, not without an occasional weed.

NANCY WILDERMUTH, MID-MISSOURI TAWL

Perspective From a TAWL Teacher

A structure of wood, cement, and stone provides a sense of security and permanence, something to lean on, and many teachers lean on that wall. Some of us become complacent about our roles, giving up control and becoming one with the structure we have leaned on so heavily. Others find the leaning uncomfortable and chafe against a surface we find cold, unyielding, and splintery. How do we let go? How do we move out of the shadow of that security to the more fragile framework of the garden trellis and risk the uncertainties of a growth process that is not identical from plant to plant or year to year? If you are comfortably complacent—or uncomfortably chafing—read with me the messages from the participants in A Day of Whole Language.

Janie Hydrick

Through the Maze

In the early days of artificial intelligence, computer scientists attempted to define intelligence in terms of what intelligent people did. The result was computers that were trivia experts and could win at chess but couldn't make their way through a unique maze or create new solutions. Similarly, in the early days of formalized reading instruction, reading "scientists" attempted to define reading competence in terms of what competent readers did. The result was children who often became phoneme experts and could win at skill drills but couldn't make their way through a semantic maze or read or write for their own purposes. I'd like to present a definition of whole language in terms of what a whole language child, my six-year-old daughter, Libby, does. The teachers at Mary Glover's Awakening Seed School in Tempe, Arizona, define its whole language curriculum in terms of what a wholly rich language environment needs to be for a language-based learner such as Libby. The result is a mode and a philosophy of learning that pervade Libby's interactions with her environment in all aspects of her life, wherever she is, whatever she is doing. Language is her way of learning, and her way of communicating what she is learning and has learned. She is nurtured in her attempts and desires to communicate, not judged by her degree of conventionality, not evaluated in terms of her conformity to models outside of herself.

Libby has long since rendered futile any of our attempts to organize her writing. I wanted her to write in a notebook so I could keep it all together and in chronological order. But Libby defies spiral bindings and gummed edges, uniformity and sequence. She writes everywhere, on anything. Any color, any size, any shape of paper is fair game. So is any color, size, or shape of pen, pencil, crayon, or marker. She is even comfortable on the word processor, where she composed this letter to her brother in the Navy:

> Dear Michael,
>   I love you. I would be sad if I did not have you in my life. wen are you kameen home - me and Kip are making a klas in the bak yard. your invidid in if you want - to Michael - from Libby.

Libby's writing comes in all forms and for all purposes. She writes lists of words or friends, telephone numbers, stories, cartoon characters with bubbles, memos, secret notes, and posters. Notes are her most prolific form of writing, and they are often most unexpected. If I open my wallet at the grocery store or unpack my suitcase when I'm traveling, I discover a note from Libby. When I arrived in Baltimore for the convention, there was a series of notes tucked in here and there among my clothes, each with its own specially made envelope. One read:

> I LOVE YOU
> YOU ARE THE BEST

Another, with the cover note

> I HOP YOU LIKT IT,

read,

> YOr GRAT

And another, with the cover note

> YOU'LL LIK THIS WON,

contained two lists of words she had spelled. One list rhymed:

> HUG
> KISS
> PENSTATE
> SIT
> KIT
> TIT

The other list did not.

BACPAC	FOOD
PEPLLE	MOMMY
DREINGK	KIPY
	DAD
	Libby

When I listen to the answering machine and make my list of messages, Libby's sitting on my lap, making her own list of the same messages.

Signs pop up all around the house. On one of the bookshelves, we saw this one:

BOOKS
RED
KERFLLY
YOUMOET
FRGET
AWRD

One sign on the television explained why the television was turned off (KLEEN UP TIM). Sometimes, television signs list characters' names, like this list from one of her favorite series, *Anne of Green Gables*:

MARILLA
AN of GReen
GABLeS
MaThYou
GILLBRT

On the refrigerator, Libby lists her chores:

Libbys CHORES
DRESS MY SELL
PUT UP PILLOWS
PICK UP
M TOYS
TOYS AND BOOKS

And right underneath the chore list is this statement of attitude:

WRK WRK
I LOVE IT
SO MACH (much)
IT MACX A
SMIL IN MY (me)

Last week there was a Post-it note on the toilet seat with this quote from one of her favorite books, *Joshua's Potty:* "And he sat and he sat and sat and sat and sat."

Her notes serve as gentle reminders to family members that there were promises made of places to go and things to do. To Oma, her grandmother, this note:

TAKE ME TO THE ZOO SOME DaY
I LOVE YOU

And the next day, a more pressing message:

ENE WAS LES
GET ON WITH THAT
I WOULLD LIKE TO GO TO
THE ZOO
(Anyways, let's get on with that. I would like to go to the zoo.)

This note was a reminder to me that I had promised her she would be the first to ride in the new van's front seat:

TO MOM FROm LIBBY
remBR YOU ;SED I
COD rID IN THE NOO
SeeT FrST

Sometimes her notes convey appreciation:

I LOVE YOU
For hep WITh
MY BaD SOr ThrOT

Sometimes her notes convey sympathy:

Libby
I love you dear mom. I am sorry kibbles is dead.

(Kibbles was my school hamster that died.)

This one was decorated with happy faces and dollar signs:

GOING TO THE MOLE
(Going to the mall)

Not all notes are sweet. This one that she slipped to me with tongue in cheek called me

SLIM FROM KOR of Teh ERTh
(slime from the core of the earth!)

One day, Libby wrote a full-page cursive letter to Oma, then turned to me and said, "What does it say, Mommy?" Trying to be as supportive as I could, I said, "You've made a lot of good cursive shapes, but it doesn't really say anything, Libby." Without- hesitation, she said, "Well, if it did say something in cursive what would it say?" Her own solution to that question was eventually to call it "kid cursive," a kind of cursive that doesn't have the same conventions as "big cursive."

Libby is definitely in control. If a book she's reading needs more words, she simply writes them in. And she's not intimidated by conventions of spelling or writing. Her dad and I were at a school-board meeting and Libby had her quiet bag, a bag filled with an assortment of paper, pencils, and books. She drew a picture of Frank's car and then whispered, "How do you spell 'this'?" When I whispered back, "t-h-i-s," she looked somewhat concerned but wrote it. More concern when "is" sounded out as "i-s." Then she came to "car" and asked how to spell it. I said, "c-a-r." She wrote "k-a-r." I whispered, "Libby, it's c-a-r." She responded, no longer whispering, "Well, it should be k-a-r. It looks better," and left it as k-a-r.

Libby knows her authors. She'll sit down and say, "I'm Marc Brown," and tell a story that sounds like Marc Brown. Or she'll say, "I'm Dr. Seuss," and tell the same story as she did for Marc Brown but make it sound as if it were written by Dr. Seuss. Libby can recite entire books and does. In the park, in the grocery store, or on a walk, we're treated to the entire text of *Whose Mouse Are You?* or *Old Mother Middle Muddle* or *Each Peach Pear Plum*. In the car, we chant *Rikki Tikki Tembo* or the chorus from *The Judge*. Libby puts on plays ranging from full, one-woman shows with advance ticket sales, posters, costumes, and backdrops to a simple, short dramatic reading.

Friends of ours have a son the same age as Libby but in public school. Libby had been reciting some of her favorite poetry to him. Not to be outdone, he said, "I know a poem," and recited "Star Light, Star Bright." Libby could hardly wait until he was done to say, "Do you really believe that? No wonder your wishes don't come true. That's not really a star at all. It's the planet Venus. I researched Venus at school. Did you know...," and proceeded to give him a full account of the planet Venus. The parent newsletter sent home on Friday during the solar system study explained to parents the controversy regarding distances of the planets from the sun. The children had researched carefully and had even contacted sources at the local university. Their conclusion was that the information, fluid and changing as it was, was not as important as the process of researching.

Probably the most humbling experience I've had was one that happened early in October. The school newsletter said that Libby's class was studying dinosaurs, fossils, and bones. In my typical overenthusiastic, nurturing-mother mode, I pulled out everything I had on bones and dinosaurs. The pile on the den floor was getting deeper and wider with books, pictures, art projects, and models. Finally, this little voice cried out, "Stop, Mommy, stop!" Libby informed me that some things were more appropriate than others, that she didn't just want stuff on dinosaurs and stuff on bones, but that she wanted stuff that would help her make a link or a connection between the two. The pile she came up with about twenty minutes later, the Libby pile, was carefully and thoughtfully selected. It was connected and it made sense.

Libby's experience in a whole language curriculum supported her natural language curiosity. It empowered her to read and write for her own purposes and to make her way through the semantic mazes of life and learning.

Perspective From a TAWL Teacher

Libby's excitement about language and learning is gratifying indeed. Can we accomplish that in all our classrooms? Do we have the freedom and knowledge, to face the challenges at the chalk face? It is a different kind of security that enables us to move away from leaning on stone structures—the growing awareness that we as teachers, students, and learners can stand on our own as we become empowered. It is a vision shared by Bess Altwerger.

Bess Altwerger

Whole Language Teachers
Empowered Professionals

When I was given this title for my presentation, I was thrilled, because I believe that this is, indeed, what we are and must be—empowered professionals. But as I considered this way of characterizing ourselves, I became concerned that we define very carefully what we mean by this label, lest it become more bravado than substance. Each word of this label has a multiplicity of meanings, used in a wide range of contexts. What, in fact, do we mean by the word *teacher* as it describes a whole language teacher? In what way is a whole language teacher a professional—like a doctor or a lawyer? Furthermore, what is an *empowered* professional in the context of being a teacher? The more I thought about it, the more I realized that my presentation should be devoted to defining the title itself—what it means to be a whole language teacher/empowered professional. I'd like to share with you my definition of each term, and in so doing, create a new potential for the whole—a new vision of what it means to be a whole language teacher.

TEACHER

The key term in our title is *teacher*, because our vision of teacher is the most fundamental issue in shifting to a whole language paradigm. Just as many of us have had to grapple with accepted images of what it means to be a good mother or a good father as we define ourselves in today's contexts, we as teachers have had to struggle with traditional images of what it means to be a good teacher as we define anew our role within whole language.

What are some characteristics of the traditional "good" teacher? First of all, the good teacher is an imparter of knowledge, a human instrument through which information is transmitted to students. In order to achieve this, the good teacher must obviously have a solid command of the subject matter to be imparted. There is no sense that knowledge is to be created with students. Rather, knowledge must be in the possession of the teacher so that, in Freire's terms (Freire, 1985), it may be "deposited" into the minds of students. This characteristic of the traditional good teacher makes many whole language teachers feel uneasy, even guilty, about exploring as colearners with students subjects about which they themselves are not fully knowledgeable.

Additionally, the good teacher approaches knowledge as politically and socially neutral. Content to be transmitted (whether in reading, writing, math, or social studies) is accepted by the good teacher, rather than interrogated on the basis of its theoretical or social value. She or he never critiques curriculum content or encourages students to do so.

Finally, the good teacher is one that can break down information and skills into digestible parts, determine the best order in which to transmit it, and do so in an orderly and logical fashion. All the while, the good teacher finds a way to keep the students motivated and interested in the subject matter.

Given this image of the good teacher, success is basically determined by the extent to which students have acquired the transmitted information and how well the teacher has controlled the students in this endeavor. Interestingly, however, the students, rather than this model of teaching, are blamed for any failure to learn. The traditional teacher is, in a sense, protected from blame for failure. And it is this fact that prevents many teachers from taking the risk of becoming a whole language teacher.

It is this transmission model of teaching that has prompted many school districts around the country to hire teachers with liberal arts backgrounds or expertise in particular subject areas regardless of their pedagogical expertise. It also underlies the appeal of mastery teaching, which ensures that even the most inexperienced teachers will passively transmit information and skills in a precise and orderly manner. And although change has begun, for the most part colleges of education are still in the business of cranking out future generations of "good" teachers, who accept, rather than challenge, the norm.

Now, if we reject this traditional image of a teacher, how shall we redefine it in the context of whole language teaching? How does it differ from what we have described?

In order to build an image of teacher in a whole language context, I have searched through my own experiences to find the teachers whom I believe this label fits, and share here their most distinguishing characteristics.

I find that, indeed, these teachers are knowledgeable individuals, capable of communicating this knowledge—who perhaps have exceptional expertise in some subject area. But this is not what sets them apart from all those other teachers I have known.

These teachers have not simply been successful at imparting knowledge to me but helped me form new categories for thinking about the information, look at something in a completely new way, and synthesize and understand better what I already knew. In short, they helped me learn how to learn, and how to do so with a critical eye.

Those that stand out encouraged critique, not neutral acceptance. They helped me to believe in myself as a learner. They communicated their confidence in me, not by denying the sometimes enormous difference in our expertise, but by appreciating, respecting, and legitimizing whatever skills and knowledge I already possessed. They challenged me to outgrow myself as I interrogated and challenged my world. They left me not with conclusive answers, but with ever more fascinating questions.

These teachers were certainly not in the business of passive transmission of digestible parts. On the contrary: It was their own skill in finding connections and relationships within and among wholes and motivating in their students an active desire to analyze, and synthesize, complex bodies of knowledge that set them apart. These teachers had goals which went beyond the classroom into an often illogical and disorderly world. They are people who are committed to improving the world, who have hope for future generations, who are morally dedicated to equality and justice. Teaching for them is not just a job, but an expression of this possibility and hope.

Some of the individuals I consider to epitomize the term *teacher*—Ken and Yetta Goodman, Dorothy Menosky—I have known personally and have had the good fortune to work with directly. Others, like Paolo Freire, Henry Giroux, and Peter McLaren, I have known primarily through the written word. But through their strong, passionate written voices they have reached me in profound ways—forever changing the way I understand the world. Many of my greatest teachers have been colleagues and friends who have given me new ways to think about a mutually shared body of knowledge and have, through example, shown me that respect for children, for learning, and for critical inquiry is the real stuff that teachers are made of.

WHOLE LANGUAGE

Before connecting our concept of teacher to whole language, I'd like first to recognize the most salient features of whole language found in the current literature and then to share some important distinctions that have helped me deepen and expand my own working definition of whole language.

First of all, we know that whole language is a theoretical perspective, one that guides and is informed by practice. The relationship between theory and practice is recursive. Our theory grows as we learn through practice; our practice grows as we learn theory.

Because of this interdependence between theory and practice, we also know that whole language can be associated with, but never be synonymous with, certain instructional strategies, materials, and methodologies. For example, whole language classrooms engage students in reading and discussing real books and other forms of written language. Students engage in journal writing, composing and publishing their own writing, and using literacy as a tool for learning content. Time is reserved for shared reading experience, conferencing with students, and reading aloud. But none of these strategies alone or in concert makes for a whole language classroom. It is the marriage of theory to these practices that determines that.

Whole language is based on a view of language and learning that recognizes the primacy and variability of meaning, the indivisibility of parts and wholes, and the interrelatedness of process, product, and purpose.

Whole language classrooms are organized around the unrelenting pursuit of meaningful, active, and purposeful learning. Children actively seek answers to their own questions, pose and solve their own problems, experiment, hypothesize, and reconstruct their own understandings. Neither students nor teachers in a whole language classroom tolerate nonsense. Written language is not to be hacked to shreds, but kept alive and whole, so that it may be utilized, enjoyed, and, most important, understood.

All of this may be viewed as a whole language basics (if we can stand the term). But in studying whole language, observing and collaborating with whole language teachers, and dialoguing with other whole language educators, I have found four distinctions with great significance in deepening and refining my understanding of whole language:

- authenticity vs. practice
- learning experiences vs. activities
- demonstration vs. modeling
- collaboration vs. control

1. Authenticity vs. Practice

I owe this distinction to my colleague and friend Carole Edelsky, who has written and spoken extensively on the notion of authenticity. As whole language educators, we can build an exhaustive list of features that characterize whole language practice. But perhaps the most essential feature of a whole language classroom is that children are engaged in authentic language use—real reading and writing rather than reading and writing exercises. Very briefly stated, real reading occurs when the reader interacts with an authentic text—one written for the purpose of communicating, in which all cuing systems are present, interdependent, and predictable; where the reader's intentions and purposes guide the process; and where meaning is created by the reader in transaction with the text. Not all instances of print permit real reading and writing.

If any of these conditions is not met—if for example, the intention and purpose of reading is determined by the teacher, the text is devoid of meaning or contains only isolated language fragments (such as flash cards), or the student is reading simply to exhibit proficiency and not to create meaning—then what you have are, at best, exercises in reading and practice in reading, but not real reading.

It is easy to see that much of what happens during language-arts block in traditional classrooms is simply practice in reading and writing, not genuine reading and writing. But where I really see the value of the authenticity-vs.-practice distinction is in fine-tuning our own whole language instruction. How much of what we do in the name of whole language strategies is practice reading and writing exercise rather than real reading and writing? How would you classify matching sentence strips to big books during shared reading experiences, using story starters to elicit writing, assigning books for literature studies, having kids make dioramas on their favorite chapter of a book? Have you ever made a diorama after you've read a book? I think it would keep us on our toes, keep us theoretically sound, if we always ask ourselves these key questions: Would real readers and writers do this? Would this ever occur outside of the classroom?

2. Learning Experiences vs. Activities

Closely related to the authenticity-vs.-practice distinction is the distinction between activities and learning experiences.

The notion of activities pervades American schools. We assign activities to children after they have read a story, provide small group activities as part of social studies or science units, or assign writing activities for creative expression. Even whole language teachers can get caught up in the activity fervor. We read a big book to a small group of children, then plan a follow-up activity such as writing a new ending to the story, or an art activity related to the story.

These activities are not inherently useless or harmful. The problem with activities is that sometimes they are just that: activities, a way of keeping kids busy, or extending a lesson because we feel somehow that we're supposed to. Often activities don't serve any meaningful or important purpose. For whole language classrooms, planning activities rather than learning experiences sets the stage for inauthentic uses of language, a focus on product rather than process, and, most important, renders whole language simply a set of cute ideas.

Perhaps an example would help us distinguish between an activity and a learning experience: Following a workshop on whole language offered in their school district, teachers became interested in innovations following shared reading—children are asked to rewrite a slightly new version of a big book following a shared reading of it. A student teacher of mine planned to engage first-grade students in rewriting the big book *Rosie's Walk* by Pat Hutchins after reading it together. She planned to rewrite the story, leaving out key words or characters so that the students could fill in with their own words, thereby creating a new version of the story. After discussing this activity, neither of us could determine its real value as a literacy learning experience. But through talking about this activity, we realized we could transform it into a learning experience by exploring a characteristic of the book that the children themselves had pointed out—the unique way in which Pat Hutchins expresses humor through illustration, reserving print for story line only. The kids did end up writing their own class big book, but for the purpose of exploring a particular literary strategy that real authors use to delight and entertain their audience.

Key questions here become: What is the purpose behind this? How does this help them learn more about reading and writing and grow as readers and writers?

3. Demonstration vs. Modeling

One of the most important principles behind whole language is that children learn not just through imitation but through engagement, hypothesis posing and testing, and social meditation with others.

Whole language theory rejects the behaviorist view of the role of adults in the learning situation. In this conception, adults provide models of the correct form, which are eventually incorporated by the learner through repeated exposure, imitation, reinforcement, and correction. The focus for the learner and the teacher is on observable surface behaviors. If flawed models are provided, the learning will be flawed. This conception of learning permeates American schooling and has left traces in all of us.

Whole language theory recognizes the crucial role of adults in the learning process. Our role is not to provide perfect models, but rather to provide demonstrations of process. Research on early literacy suggests that adults support literacy development through providing demonstrations of the reading and writing processes. We demonstrate the myriad comprehension strategies, albeit unconsciously, as we read to our children at home, and we demonstrate the uses of writing in our society as we write in the presence of our children. Providing demonstrations rather than models for children is the goal of a whole language curriculum.

Returning to our example of the innovation activity, we can see that the original plan was simply to use literature as a model for writers to imitate. In transforming it into a learning experience, students developed insights into the process of authorship. Demonstration of process became the focus of the learning.

We must ask ourselves daily the key question: What does this reveal to students about what real readers and writers do with language processes?

4. Collaboration vs. Control

Some classrooms that have most impressed parents, administrators, and other teachers as examples of whole language classrooms have left me uneasy. Yes, they may have had almost every visible marker of a whole language classroom—the highly literate environment, the focus on comprehension and composing, the immersion in literature. The teacher may have used every whole language strategy imaginable—literature studies, shared reading, conferencing, themes. But what made me uneasy was something intangible, something not immediately obvious—except perhaps in the perfection of the classroom itself.

A genuine whole language classroom must belong to both the students and the teacher. Children's ideas, purposes, and questions are the driving force of the classroom. In these classrooms the bulletin boards are less polished and elaborate—because they've been developed by the students, serve students' purposes, and display students' work. The class-made big books may not be museum pieces, because they have not been written by the teacher but rather written and illustrated by the children themselves. The committee work generated by groups of children as they study some theme (maps, charts, reports, art projects) may lack the customary glitter and polish, because learning—not the products themselves—was the focus of the activities.

The classrooms that make me uneasy are those that are too perfect, because the perfection is a reflection of teacher control rather than collaboration. Locked into past beliefs about what makes a good teacher, we spend hours after school making perfect bulletin boards and planning literature units before the children even read the books. We spend our summer vacations planning elaborate thematic units, finding all the materials we'll need, before we even meet our children and find out what they already know or care to know about the subject. Whole language classrooms include children in the entire learning process, from posing the questions to planning learning experiences to finding materials to encoding their knowledge. What separates a real whole language classroom from a fancy facsimile is not how many typical whole language strategies can be found there in one day, but the extent to which learning has become truly collaborative.

Our key question here becomes: Is the curriculum developed through a collaborative effort of teacher *and* students, reflecting all interests, questions, and purposes?

WHOLE LANGUAGE TEACHER

We've defined whole language and we've defined teacher, but as Ken Goodman and Frank Smith have taught us, the meaning of the whole language teacher incorporates but also transcends the individual meanings of *whole language* and *teacher*. A whole language teacher is much more than just a teacher implementing a whole language approach in the classroom.

First and foremost, a whole language teacher is a learner—one who has taken great risks to grow in his/her beliefs about teaching and learning, one who continues to take risks every day of his/her professional life. They are individuals who are exhilarated about learning and can communicate this zeal to their students. I have never met a real whole language teacher who is bored in the classroom. Using their students as informants (as Jerry Harste and Yetta Goodman would urge them to do), whole language teachers are continually learning more about the learning process, critically evaluating new ideas against their professional knowledge, and finding ways to incorporate this new learning into their instructional practice. They are willing and eager to ask themselves the critical questions outlined above in order to ensure that their practice remains consistent with their beliefs. And they are willing to reconsider practice if their answers come up short. Yes, whole language teachers are learners—reflective and critical learners, willing to take risks in order to grow.

Whole language teachers also have an unwavering respect, appreciation, and acceptance of their students. They love their students—but not in the sentimental sense against which Freire cautions us. Their love lacks any hint of pity and despair. Rather it is an optimistic love—one that leads them to find strength and competence in all students. They see their jobs as building on the knowledge and abilities their students already have, not in making up for what they lack.

Whole language teachers are more than just skilled practitioners. They are exceedingly knowledgeable individuals who can explain and defend their practice. Because whole language is not simply a set of methods but theory in practice, whole language teachers must understand theory in order to practice. And perhaps most important, they have a hand in the continual development of the theory through their practice. Whole language theory is not generated through controlled laboratory experiments and then applied to the world of the classroom, but rather it results from critical inquiry into how real children learn in natural environments and how language operates in genuine language contexts. Because whole language theory is not alienated from practice, it remains dynamic and evolving—and responsive to the world of practice. Whole language teachers are themselves researchers, who contribute to the theory which we as a community of learners build together.

PROFESSIONAL

In response to the "de-skilling" of teaching that has insidiously crept into our educational system over the years, teachers today are demanding that they be regarded as professionals, not just technicians or clerks. I wholeheartedly join others in insisting that we teachers be treated with the respect we deserve. But I believe that we should be cautious in defining the term *professional*. What does it mean to be a professional in the context of being a whole language educator?

I believe that when we use this term to describe teachers, we are enlisting certain images of professionals that we all admire—images of competency, autonomy in decision making, intelligence, respect from others. But we need to be careful that in describing ourselves as professionals and living out that role, we do not assume the less admirable characteristics of professionals in other fields. Allow me first to describe the characteristics that I believe we should try our best to avoid and then to redefine professional in the context of a whole language teacher.

The role of professional carries with it a level of status in our society. This status, in some sense, is well deserved—after all, professionals often work hard and long to develop their expertise. But as we all know from our contact with certain doctors or lawyers, professionals sometimes adopt an attitude of superiority and elitism that we as teachers must avoid. This elitism is dangerous because it destroys any spirit of cooperation and mutual respect between the professionals and those seeking their services. Instead it fosters a system of intimidation that renders the client or patient powerless and shields the professional from criticism. Perhaps most important, when professionals view themselves as an elite segment of society, they become resistant to growth and transformation as they steadfastly protect their image of perfection and superiority.

If teachers buy into the role of professional as elite worker, we run the risk of alienating our students and communities as we gain power at their expense and work against them as antagonists rather than with them as allies. Furthermore, our profession will cease to grow if we are unwilling to undergo self-evaluation and critique. This is antithetical to the spirit of whole language and inconsistent with our view of teachers as learners.

If we set aside this view of professionals, how then are whole language teachers professionals? Whole language teachers are professionals in the sense that we are not just trained to perform the job of teaching but are educated, knowledgeable, and capable of making important decisions regarding our teaching. We resist recent efforts to liken the role of teacher to that of factory workers, who, in this society, are alienated from all decisions regarding the nature of their work and who are rewarded only for efficiency, complicity, and passivity. In this society, the label of professional is applied only to workers who possess the knowledge they need to make informed decisions, whose judgment is valued and respected, not dismissed as irrelevant or, at best, subjective. As whole language teachers, we are reclaiming our right to make important educational decisions regarding our students and our programs. The professionals in education are not just sitting in the publishing houses in New York or in the Educational Testing Service in New Jersey; they are right inside the classroom, living day to day with students, learning who they are as individuals, and assessing their growth as readers and writers. Yes, whole language teachers are professionals, in the best sense of the term.

EMPOWERED

Let's turn now to the term *empowered*. Besides the term *whole language* itself, I think that the term *empower* must be eligible for an award for being the most used, misused, and abused term in education today. It has almost become educationally fashionable to call for the empowerment of teachers and students. But empowerment can refer to everything from letting teachers choose among three basal programs for their classroom to allowing students to self-select books for SSR time. I'm not claiming that there is, in fact, only one meaning for the term. But because there is a wide range of meanings for it, we need to define it in the context of the whole language teacher as a professional. What does it mean to say that whole language teachers are not just professionals but empowered professionals? What difference does the term empowered make to the meaning of the entire label? I'd like to share with you my own thoughts on this, because it is vitally important to how we view ourselves in the entire educational process.

The first level of meaning that the term empowered has had for me is the personal. That is, individuals can become personally empowered, finding the inner strength to determine the course of their own lives and taking control over the major decisions that affect their lives. To me, becoming empowered connotes that some transformation has occurred, personal liberation from some formerly dominating force—another person, a group. The empowered individual has achieved empowerment through personal struggle—it hasn't been handed to him or her as a gift.

When we apply this personal meaning of empowerment to whole language teachers, it means that we as individuals have taken control over our own professional lives—that we are no longer personally willing to yield to external demands and expectations that we believe not to be in the best interest of our students. It means that we have found our voices, no longer willing to resort to covert teaching—to writing one plan and teaching quite another. For many of us it means finding our voices through the written word. Never before have so many articles written by classroom teachers appeared in professional journals. For others of us it means believing enough in our own expertise that we are willing to conduct workshops and speak at conferences—this conference, IRA, and local TAWL conferences around the country.

For those of us who are women, becoming an empowered professional has meant a day-to-day personal struggle to contradict the sexist stereotyping of teachers as passive, less skilled, and temporary. It has meant, for many of us, the struggle to approach male administrators or local school boards as competent, capable, and knowledgeable professionals. For those of you who are men, becoming an empowered professional has surely meant convincing yourselves and others that being a nurturing, caring teacher is as appropriate and valuable a career as other more male-dominated professions. For minorities and the working class, professional empowerment has perhaps meant overcoming the sense of powerlessness and alienation once felt as students in the very system in which we've chosen to lead our professional lives. And for all of us, it has meant overcoming the negative images of teachers portrayed in the media—to become proud to say that we have chosen to teach for our livelihood.

Personal empowerment is indeed one very crucial step in the process of becoming an empowered professional. But if we were to leave it at that, we would accomplish nothing beyond our own individual lives. We would develop no sense of mission as a collective group of whole language educators. We must ask ourselves, What are we empowered to do? What is our ultimate goal, beyond personal fulfillment?

An obvious answer would be to eradicate illiteracy, to help create a generation of children who are not just able to read and write, but who appreciate and enjoy the written word. Beyond that perhaps our goal is to help every one of our students achieve personal empowerment—to attain the same sense of self-worth that we as teachers have achieved through whole language. But I ask you to consider for a moment the world that our students will enter. Is this society one that will nurture our students' personal empowerment, one in which each of our students will have an equal opportunity to flourish and grow? As teachers, can we ignore that according to Peter McLaren, in his powerful book *Life in Schools* (McLaren, 1989), "a black infant born within five miles of the White House is more likely to die in the first year of life than an infant born in Third World countries like Trinidad" (*Time*, 1987, reported on p. 3), that "homicide coupled with suicide constitutes the sixth leading cause of death" (p. 7), that "teenage homicide is up more than 200 percent since 1960" (p. 7), that 50 to 80 percent of all inner-city students drop out or are pushed out of high school (p. 8), that by September 1987, 25 percent of the childhood population was from families who live in poverty (p. 11), that "black children of two-parent families are twice as likely as white children in two-parent families to live below the poverty line" (p. 14), and that, "in fact, almost half of all black children are poor compared to one in six white children" (p. 14)? Can we ignore the growing homeless population and unemployment rate, especially for minorities? Can we as empowered professionals ignore the social realities of our society and, most important, the role that schools play in the "legitimization of inequality" (to use McLaren's words) through testing, tracking, and standardizing curriculum? I believe that we cannot and must not.

We as whole language teachers must develop a sense of social empowerment that reaches beyond our own individuality, our own classrooms, and our own schools. We as a group must adopt as our ultimate goal the eradication of social inequality and injustice, and work to create an educational system that transforms, rather than reproduces and perpetuates, these societal conditions. We must recognize our moral obligation to our students to do more than just make them literate. We must resist efforts to reduce critical thinking to politically and socially vacuous thinking skills but engage our students in the critique of real-life issues so that they will be able to tackle societal problems that will face them in the future as they transform and improve our society. Whole language can be more than a pedagogy of language and literacy—it can be, in Giroux's words, the "pedagogy of possibility and hope" (Giroux, 1988).

WHOLE LANGUAGE TEACHERS: EMPOWERED PROFESSIONALS

We now have the whole title: "Whole Language Teachers: Empowered Professionals." We have defined each part in the context of the whole. But still our meaning for the whole is incomplete. We have not yet captured the full spirit of what it means to be a Whole Language Teacher: Empowered Professional. For this we need to think of real people we know, that we have worked with and learned from, who epitomize for us the essence of this title. For me, it is my dear friend and whole language educator Barbara Flores, who as a child was made to sit in the back of her classroom because she was a Chicana, but who today works to improve the life of Hispanic as well as other children, through speaking to teachers around the country about the strength of minority children—and has even been invited back to speak in the same school district that segregated and alienated her as a child. Or my friend and former student Elizabeth Saavedra, who also struggled long and hard to overcome society's image of Hispanic women as compliant and passive, and to believe in her heart that she truly is the brilliant and powerful woman I always knew she was. It is Bob Wortman, a former kindergarten teacher and now principal of a Tucson school, and Eddie Corona, Albuquerque Public Schools teacher, who have redefined for their students and colleagues what it really means to be a male professional—someone who links competence, professionalism, and commitment to tenderness, compassion, and sincerity. There are so many others I can name—all unique in their own way—but what they all have in common is that they are whole language educators, personally and socially empowered professionals making a difference for children and the world in which they live.

I'd like to add to our evolving image another characteristic of Whole Language Teachers: Empowered Professionals. With all our warmth, we are a tough bunch. We're intolerant of attempts to discredit whole language by characterizing it as a romantic view of education or a fad. We aren't fooled by publishers who label everything from basal programs to phonics materials "Whole Language" if there is even the slightest focus on meaning or comprehension. We are educators who can argue on theoretical and practical grounds for our position, who not only know what we believe, but why we believe it, and who are therefore able and willing to dispute these claims and accusations.

Finally, and perhaps most importantly, we are passionate advocates of children, who won't accept the image of professionals as removed, indifferent, objective. There is no place for such professionals in the lives of children. Yes, we feel strongly about our beliefs, because we know that what we are doing makes a difference—we see readers and writers where there once were failures and active, thoughtful learners where there once were bored or angry faces. We hear fascinating questions where there once were pat answers, and communities of learners where there once were only occupied classrooms.

What is a Whole Language Teacher: Empowered Professional? Look around you: There are fifteen hundred of us here today on the road to becoming one, fifteen hundred of us who have taken a whole day out of our busy schedules, and even some money out of our pockets, in order to learn, share, and grow with one another. A wall has come down in Europe, but together we are taking down some invisible walls of our own. I hope this day will help you find the motivation and inspiration you need to get the job done. Thank you.

REFERENCES

Freire, P. *The Politics of Education.* Granby, Massachusetts: Bergin & Garvey Publishers, Inc., 1985.

Giroux, H. *Teachers as Intellectuals.* Granby, Massachusetts: Bergin & Garvey Publishers, Inc., 1988.

McLaren, P. *Life in Schools.* New York: Longman, 1989.

Bess Altwerger is a faculty member at Towson State University in Towson, Maryland.

Perspective From a TAWL Teacher

It can be a heady feeling—professional empowerment! It is also a growth process, uniquely challenging for each whole language teacher who moves away from the security of stone walls for the fragile warmth of the garden trellis. Come share the metamorphosis of friends and colleagues.

KITTYE COPELAND AND DOROTHY WATSON

The Odyssey of Two Whole Language Teachers
WHAT WE'VE LEARNED FROM EACH OTHER AND FROM OUR STUDENTS

DOROTHY: We've come to share with you our odyssey of learning together, how the two of us, with the support of our TAWL group, have grown as whole language teachers. Our presentation has to do with those people, events, and lessons that have contributed to us as two whole language teachers—two whole language learners—becoming free to learn together.

We must first recognize the group of teachers who for twelve years have supported and encouraged our learning and growth. These Teachers Applying Whole Language have given us strength and friendship. Our TAWL group appears throughout our presentation.

KITTYE: Literature has also supported us, empowered us, and given us direction. When we started talking about this presentation, our friend and colleague Paul Crowley suggested that we look at literature—possibly poetry—for help in telling our story and demonstrating our belief in partnership.

DOROTHY: We found in Paul Fleischman's Newberry Award-winning book *Joyful Noise: Poems for Two Voices* the perfect metaphor for our growth as whole language teachers, especially in his poem "Chrysalis Diary." Come share Paul Fleischman's poem and reflect on your personal odyssey into whole language.

"CHRYSALIS DIARY" BY PAUL FLEISCHMAN

November 13:

Cold told me
to fasten my feet
to this branch,
to dangle upside down
from my perch,
to shed my skin,
to cease being a caterpillar
and I have obeyed.
and I have obeyed.

December 6:

Green,
the color of leaves and life,
has vanished!
has vanished!
The empire of leaves
lies in ruins!
lies in ruins!
I study the
brown new world around me.
I fear the future.

I hear few sounds.
Have any others of my kind
survived this cataclysm?
Swinging back and forth
in the wind,
I feel immeasurably alone.

January 4:
I can make out snow falling.
For five days and nights
it's been drifting down.
I find I never tire of
watching the flakes
in their multitudes
passing my window.
The world is now white.
Astounding.
Astounding.
I enter these
wondrous events
in my chronicle
knowing no reader
would believe me.

February 12:
An ice storm last night.
Unable to see out
at all this morning.
Yet I hear boughs cracking
and branches falling.
Hungry for sounds
in this silent world,
I cherish these,
ponder their import,
miser them away
in my memory,
and wait for more.
and wait for more.

March 28:
I wonder if
I am the same being
who started this diary.
I've felt stormy inside
like the weather without.
My mouth is reshaping,
my legs are dissolving,
wings are growing
my body's not mine.
my body's not mine.
This morning,
a breeze from the south,
strangely fragrant,
a red-winged blackbird's
call in the distance,
a faint glimpse of green
in the branches.
And now I recall
that last night
I dreamt of flying.

KITTYE: Just as we ask our students to feel the patterns, the images, the symbols that connect with their lives and consequently bring power to the reading of stories, we felt Paul Fleischman's metaphor. Come share:

OUR CHRYSALIS DIARY

(See Figures 1 and 2.)

June 1976:

DOROTHY: We meet in a summer class with summer ways.

KITTYE: I come, a teacher, a twelve-year veteran. I'm on the fringes, near burnout. I'll give it one more try.

DOROTHY: I come, eager to learn from teachers who bring the immediacy of their experiences, the honesty of their concern, the freshness of their ideas.

WE ARE SURE OF ONE THING. IT IS AN IMPORTANT TIME IN OUR LIVES.

KITTYE: My file cabinets are filled with worksheets—from alphabetic dot-to-dots to copy the word to circle the short vowel sounds.

DOROTHY: Our inquiry begins.

KITTYE: All my skill practices come rushing headfirst against solid research findings in this class about children's reading and writing.

NATURALLY.

DOROTHY: Theory must be confirmed and enriched by teachers who are immersed in the dynamics of learning. I must learn from those whose inner wisdom comes from watching and listening to children learn.

NATURALLY.
THE CLASS ENDS. WE GO OUR SEPARATE WAYS.

KITTYE: I feel immeasurably alone.

DOROTHY: I feel immeasurably alone.

(See Figure 3.)

September 1977:

THERE IS A NEED.

KITTYE: Within the classroom the children and I work together. We take risks, we learn, we grow. The magic is there. I must share the experience.

THERE IS A NEED.

DOROTHY: Within my classes the students and I talk together about taking risks, making choices, being liberated. I must confirm the experiences.

THERE IS A NEED

KITTYE: For colleagues,

DOROTHY: for friends

TO COME TOGETHER

KITTYE: to share successes,

DOROTHY: adventures,

KITTYE: language stories,

DOROTHY: and literacy lessons.

TAWL IS FORMED.

DOROTHY: We study.

KITTYE: We question.

DOROTHY: We practice.

KITTYE: We share our concerns, our doubts. Together we can research and learn.

DOROTHY: Together we can be scared

KITTYE: and brave.

TOGETHER.
WE ENTER THESE WONDROUS EVENTS IN OUR CHRONICLES.

Research and Inquiry

August 1980:

A NEED

KITTYE: To check our theory,

DOROTHY: to study our practices.

KITTYE: Collaboratively, we explore my first-grade room.

DOROTHY: We risk, we explore.

WE ARE VULNERABLE.

DOROTHY: The children are our informants.

KITTYE: We explore our whole language curriculum.

DOROTHY: The children direct our thoughts.

KITTYE: We explore our theory.

DOROTHY: The children assure us.

KITTYE: Our research confirms what other researchers, theorists, and teachers suggest.

DOROTHY: We confirm.

KITTYE: We grow.

TOGETHER.

WE CHERISH THESE, PONDER THEIR IMPORT.

Rewards

February 1982:

DOROTHY: A telegram informs us that the International Reading Association's Nila Banton Smith Award winner is Kittye Copeland.

KITTYE: I am selected—a whole language teacher!

WE ARE ECSTATIC—WE CELEBRATE.

DOROTHY: Our theory is validated.

KITTYE: Our practices are valued. Reading and writing are transactional across all the curriculum. Even in first grade.

(See Figure 4.)

And Punishment

KITTYE: Have any others of my kind

DOROTHY: survived this cataclysm?

October 1982:

KITTYE: The descent from the mountaintop.

DOROTHY: Do whole language teachers have to suffer?

KITTYE: I did.

BUT NOT ALONE.

DOROTHY: Apparently, sound practices need defending.

KITTYE: Should I recant? Give up what I've worked so hard to learn? Be passive? Act submissive?

IS IT WORTH THE GRIEF?

KITTYE: The school-board meeting is called.

DOROTHY: Kittye dresses in black.

KITTYE: Dorothy dresses in red.

THE TAWL TEACHERS ARRIVE DRESSED IN COLORS OF THE RAINBOW.

November 1982:

DOROTHY: A breeze from the south.

KITTYE: A faint glimpse of green.

DOROTHY: The parents respond with eloquent praise. If there can be winners in such situations...

(See Figure 5.)

WE WIN

KITTYE: At the end of the year I resign to teach in a whole language environment, one that respects teachers as decision makers and values students as intelligent learners.

DOROTHY: The rest of the story: August 1989, seven years after the school-board trial, that *complaining parent* calls to ask a local tutorial service for help with her youngest child. She wants him to be tutored in whole language.

KITTYE: Oblivious to my pain.

THROUGH THE YEARS

KITTYE: We flourish. Our TAWL group grows from six to one hundred.

DOROTHY: Our Renewal Conference from forty to seven hundred. We come to know and to learn from

KITTYE: storytellers, researchers, theorists, and writers,

DOROTHY: leading the way,

KITTYE: sometimes shaking in our boots, but firm in our convictions because our students have informed us, our students have empowered us, our students have set us free.

THE CREDIBILITY GAP IS CLOSING.

KITTYE: We grow professionally.

DOROTHY: Excuse us for bragging, but

KITTYE: our fame is spreading beyond our borders. We have the opportunity to share our knowledge, experience, and enthusiasm.

DOROTHY: Whole language theory and practice.

KITTYE: Those teachers are good at it!

DOROTHY: For in-services, workshops, seminars, speeches...

KITTYE: bring in those whole language teachers!
WE'RE ON THE ROAD.
WE TALK, WE SING, WE MISCUE, WE BIG BOOK, WE THEME AND SCHEME, WE PROCESS-WRITE, WE LOG, WE JOURNAL, WE RE-SEARCH, WE INQUIRE, WE EVALUATE! WE LIBERATE!

DOROTHY: We're good!

KITTYE: They love us!

DOROTHY: And then!

(See Figure 6.)

WE BOMB! THEY HATE US!

DOROTHY: We whimper.

KITTYE: We lick our wounds.

WE FEAR THE FUTURE.

DOROTHY: We cry.

KITTYE: We talk.

DOROTHY: We reevaluate.

KITTYE: We start over.

TOGETHER.

KITTYE: Wings are growing.

(See Figure 7.)

KITTYE: February 1989:

THE WHOLE LANGUAGE UMBRELLA

DOROTHY: Whole language teachers around the world.

KITTYE: An idea whose time has come.

DOROTHY: And that idea comes from the heads and hearts of teachers from Wollengong to Winnipeg to Wichita.

KITTYE: Grass roots. Teachers talking to teachers. Educators of all ages, all grades, all categories, all learners.

DOROTHY: TAWL groups emerge. Teachers Applying

KITTYE: or Attempting

DOROTHY: Whole Language.

A NEED

KITTYE: to share with others across the continent—around the world.

DOROTHY: Where can I talk to another fourth-grade teacher?

KITTYE: Where can I go for help with writing workshops?

DOROTHY: Where can I see a school that has survived transition?

KITTYE: What should I read?

DOROTHY: If I reach out,

KITTYE: there *will be* someone to help!

THE WHOLE LANGUAGE UMBRELLA
A NETWORK OF GROUPS AND INDIVIDUALS WHO ARE DEDICATED
TO A STUDENT CENTERED, MEANING FOCUSED, LITERATURE-
FILLED CURRICULUM.

DOROTHY: Our constitution is ratified.

KITTYE: Our advisory board chosen.

WE DID IT WITH YOU—TOGETHER.

ADDITIONS TO OUR DIARY

DOROTHY: Kittye, what were your first steps into the study of whole language research and theory?

KITTYE: My students supported and confirmed my early understandings, as reading miscue analysis informed me about the reading process. As I listened to my students read, I began to see that when readers transact with rich text, they can construct meaning independent of the teacher. As Lara read from *Little Women,* she came to the word *Hummels* in the sentence "Meg, I wish you'd go and see the Hummels...." She stopped reading and said, "Oh, I know what that word is. Those are little clay figures of German characters." As a reader, I thought *Hummel* was the name of a family, but I didn't question Lara; she could be right. She continued to read, and encountering the word again, she miscued. Instead of reading, "It's well enough for me to go out with Meg, but not well enough *to go to the* Hummels," Lara read, "*to get the* Hummels." It confirmed for me that indeed the text was talking about a family, but still Lara believed *Hummel* was a figurine. Again, I allowed Lara to move ahead in the text in order to confirm or disconfirm her notion. Reading on, she came to the word again, but this time the text provided another cue, *Mrs. Hummel.* Realizing that *Hummel* was not a figurine, Lara said, "Oh, this is a name of a family." The text and the reader came together, without teacher interference.

Another student, Kate, wrote a letter to me seeking clarification of a portion of the text. The children frequently wrote notes to each other and to me and mailed them in our classroom post office. Kate wanted to clear up some things that couldn't wait until time for the literature study group to meet:

(See Figure 8.)

In addition to my marginal notes to Kate, I circled the word *explore* and added a question mark; I wasn't sure what Kate was writing about. Kate replied:

(See Figure 9.)

Knowing Kate's relationship with her grandmother, I understood that when she read about Aunt March, she was thinking of her grandmother, bringing her personal meaning to the text. As a collaborative reader with Kate, I offered her my interpretation of the story.

In our class, children talk a great deal about literature outside of their literature discussion circles. It isn't unusual to hear kids say, "You're acting just like Ramona." Through well-loved books, Ramona has almost become a member of the class.

DOROTHY: Many of our lessons had to do with the uses of language and the power of that usage. M.A.K. Halliday tells us that we learn a language, we learn about that language, and we learn about life through using language. Using language a great deal in authentic ways (student-chosen writing, real literature) doesn't "use up" language or wear out the user; using language in inauthentic ways (filling in blanks, reading meaningless text) not only exhausts the language but exhausts the user as well. As students validate Halliday's theories, we learn to value authentic curriculum.

Kittye, you've conducted research in your classroom that supports Halliday's theory. How is the trustworthy literacy curriculum evident in your classroom?

KITTYE: I have been generalizing Halliday's theory about learning language as you use language. I noticed that children who started in our classroom approached writing in a more positive and proficient way than those who came from textbook-driven programs. I developed a questionnaire to get a sense of children's attitudes that affected their approach to writing.

The following examples of two students were typical of the differences in attitude. Eric has spent years in a conventional skills-based classroom. Lara has always been in a whole language setting.

(See Figures 10, 11, and 12.)

Eric, a fourth-grader who just came in September, chose this as his best piece of writing:

(See Figure 13.)

Lara, a fifth-grader who had been in our whole language program since kindergarten, chose this as her favorite piece:

(See Figure 14.)

As learners from opposing curricular experiences, these two children view and value writing in different ways. Eric writes for his teachers and may find writing personally useful some day. Lara writes for herself and other valued audiences and finds writing meaningful and useful right now.

DOROTHY: Our chronicles are filled with stories about our students and excerpts from their own transition diaries. We listen and learn from them.

In my undergraduate class, Methods of Teaching Reading, the students keep two journals. In one they respond to class-related activities, writing about class discussions, readings, assignments, pen-pal letters, and school in general. The other is a roving journal, passed among six class members and reflecting the needs and the concerns of the writers in the group. Listen to Laura, a first-semester senior who will soon be doing her student teaching, as she writes:

> I was in the high reading group from first grade right on through sixth. It was no big deal because for the most part the good readers were left alone. We got to read a lot of books—the bad news is that I had to write a book report after each book, so I never read as many books as I could have, or wanted to. But the real problem with the reading groups was that my first great love, Denny, was in the slow reading group. Although Denny never said a word about it, I think he knew he was thought of as a lousy reader, therefore thought of as a lousy student, therefore as a lousy person—and too often he did his best to live up to his label.
>
> What I remember most vividly is that I was embarrassed for Denny. I hated that he had to do put and buh drills and to meet in a reading group every day with "the dummies." The absolute worst day of my life was when Mrs. Clairmore paired Denny and me to do his flash cards. He struggled and I died. I think that may have been the first time in my entire life I ever doubted that I wanted to grow up to be a teacher. It never crossed my mind that there was a real alternative to labeling kids, assigning them to reading groups, and then drilling and skilling the poor readers.
>
> Now I know that there is a more humane and joyful way of teaching kids to read and write—a way that comes out of good research with real kids. I'm so sorry and just a bit angry that it's come too late for Denny. Thank God it's not too late for me, and, Mrs. Clairmore, wherever you are, I pray that it's not too late for you!

KITTYE: We listen and learn from our students and enter these lessons in our chrysalis diary. Dorothy and I learn from all of our students, such as Laura, who learned from her own past experiences. We also learn from the stories of authors, who relate their experiences as early readers and writers. Beverly Cleary confirmed our beliefs:

> The class had been divided into three groups: Bluebirds, who found happiness in seats by the window; Redbirds, who sat in the middle seats; and Blackbirds, who sat by the blackboard, far from sunlight. I was not surprised to be a Blackbird.
>
> The worst part of the day was the reading circle, where the Blackbirds in turn had to read words from the despised and meaningless word lists: shad, shed, shod, shin, shun, shut, shot, ship, shop, shift, shell. We all feared and hated our turns at that circle of chairs in the front of the room as much as we dreaded trying to say the words on flash cards Miss Falb held up in front of the class. With luck, *party* or *mamma*, words I could read, were flashed at me. Oh, the relief!
>
> *A Girl From Yamhill: A Memoir, page 80*

DOROTHY: Undergraduate students, in their first personal narrative writing, "How I Learned to Read and Write," reflect on their early literacy experiences. After the students write their pieces, they share one special memory with the class. The excerpts are duplicated for sharing and reflection by all, veteran and future teachers alike. Jill writes:

> We would sit cross-legged in a circle and recite the letters of the alphabet, each child calling out the next letter in turn. *E* was the hardest to remember. It seemed like a nonletter to me, an empty space rather than a sound. In the first grade, vowels drove me nuts. Who pronounces noises anyway? When I didn't know what it was, I learned to call it the schwa. Mrs. Atterbury loved the schwa.

From Elizabeth:

> I quickly separated school reading from fun reading. Although I usually did very well with the basals, I never

enjoyed them. The stories didn't interest me. The workbook was a lot of busy work. On the other hand, I loved to read library books on my own. Ramona Quimby was my good friend. I read all of Beverly Cleary's books, and when I got older, too big to go to the library and ask for them myself, I had my little sister check them out.

From Lisa:

When I was in preschool, my mom and I drove past a sign at the shopping mall. It said K-MART PLAZA. Mom recalls me reading it, saying, "Oh, good, Mom, K-Mart has pizza now."

From Kathy:

I'll never forget my first genuine writing. My mother encouraged me to write to the Avon cosmetic company about this marvelous idea I had. I had an inspiration for a lipstick color. It would be pinkish-reddish-orangish in color, and I would call it Sunset. I wrote to the Avon company, and they responded with a 'thank you very much for your idea, we'll keep it in mind' letter, and they enclosed a bottle of cologne in the shape of an ice cream soda. I was thrilled, and I was a writer for life.

From Carrie:

Well, my one memory of writing in kindergarten is a letter that we wrote to our parents. We copied it exactly from the board, and I had absolutely no idea what it said. We even walked to the post office and mailed the letters. I had no idea what I was doing. For all I knew, we were on an afternoon hike, and we put papers in a mailbox. I didn't know they were going somewhere. Needless to say, I was surprised when my mom told me she had received my letter in the mail. Is this an example of a bogus activity that *looks* authentic? My schooling is full of them.

From Kathleen:

> My dad was an avid reader. I remember him taking me to the library and saying, "Kathleen, go on, pick out any book you want." Well, to me, this was so thrilling, because even though I couldn't read all that well, my dad still encouraged me to pick out any book that I wanted, and he would help me read it.

DOROTHY: One of the first things that we notice in your classroom, Kittye, is that kids are making decisions, important ones. At one level they are deciding what to put on the bulletin board and when to sharpen their pencils, but they're also making decisions about what they are going to spend their time and energy studying. Curriculum is not a decision made only by the teacher. How do your students' decisions influence curriculum?

KITTYE: Children have input and choices. Instead of the teacher or the textbook mandating topics in science and social studies, for example, we brainstorm ideas that the children want to investigate. After they suggest any topic they want, we talk about, then vote on the suggestions to determine the top three areas of interest. On the example ballot below, the children made their first, second, and third choices, expressing their reasons for choosing each topic. Eric's first choice was to study weather; his second selection was "free choice," meaning you pick any topic you want to research, it doesn't have to be within a thematic unit; and his third choice was space.

(See Figure 15.)

Jack tells why he made his choices. His first choice was weather, his second choice was "free choice," and his third choice was space.

(See Figure 16.)

At that time, the papers were filled with news about earthquakes in California and hurricanes in Texas. It's obvious that both boys were following current events closely.

DOROTHY: Jack and Eric are about nine years old. You also have very young children in your nongraded class, five-year-olds and six-year-olds. How do these younger children get involved in research and inquiry?

KITTYE: From the very beginning of their research, the children are encouraged to write notes in their own words about something that they find important or interesting. Jack noted ideas about the barberfish that he finds interesting:

(See Figure 17.)

After a great deal of research, note taking, and talking, the learners write their reports. These are then presented orally to the other children. Jack's report shows how he puts the notes in his own words:

(See Figure 18.)

As students give their reports, the other children take notes on each presentation. Aaron and Chandler, each six years old, take notes on a report:

(See, Figure 19.)

DOROTHY: Kittye, Jack's report shows us that he is obviously comfortable with expository writing, but what about other genres? Can your students take ownership and make their voices heard in other writing modes?

KITTYE: In our program authentic writing is a daily presence. Jack plays with language when writing to a pen pal.

(See Figures 20 and 21.)

When he was sports editor of our class newspaper, Jack changed his language and style.

(See Figure 22.)

Now, Jack becomes a historian reporting on an Italian Renaissance poet.

(See Figure 23.)

Jack shifts to fiction to entertain his readers. In all cases, he has a real and specific purpose for his writing.

(See Figure 24.)

DOROTHY: Many entries in our diaries have to do with whole language assessment. Kittye, how do you evaluate in your classroom?

KITTYE: We are inviting children to focus on evaluating their own efforts. Assessment forms reflecting the goals of each literary event help children evaluate their literature study groups, their reports, and their own writings. When Gary evaluated his participation, you'll notice he gave himself a zero on writing in his literature journal.

(See Figure 25.)

Other students agreed with Gary's perceptions: "The discussion was good today because..." and "We could have had a better discussion if we would have..." Learners support and confirm each other's self-evaluations.

(See Figures 26 and 27.)

In the next literature study session, you can be sure Gary had the best written reactions.

DOROTHY: Are the students comfortable with this kind of self-evaluation?

KITTYE: I have seen the children's honesty in their evaluations, and it helps them grow. They know their strengths and their needs. At the end of the year we ask the children to think about their best work and what they could have improved. Adam is a first-grade-age child. When asked to explain what he thought was his best work and where he would like to have done better, he wrote:

(See Figure 28.)

It's interesting that the three reports that Adam had listed, I as teacher also chose as his top work. In the fall when Adam returned to school and was asked to set his new goals, he felt he needed to improve his literature response reactions. I had also chosen literature response reactions as the area needing the most improvement. We confirmed each others' evaluations.

DOROTHY: It probably isn't news that when it comes to some aspects of whole language it's far easier to preach than to practice. That's true for me in my undergraduate Methods of Teaching Reading class. But I've tried in small ways to move the students into the kind of self-evaluation that we find in Kittye's classroom. One of our whole language first-grade teachers, Sandy Nichols, modified an idea from Kenneth Koch's book *Wishes, Lies, and Dreams.* Sandy invites her children, even on the first day of school, to write, "I used to...but now" poetry, from *Wishes, Lies, and Dreams.* Here is an excerpt of that poem from Sandy's first-grade class. This from Ted:

> I used to be scared of school
> But now I've been in first grade for a whole day.

Other teachers tried it. From John, a seventh-grade special-education student:

> I used to think I couldn't write
> But now I know I'm an author. (In fact, I'm a poet!)

From a second-grade teacher:

> I used to think I could grade papers while my students
> wrote,
> But now I know they need to see me writing and need
> to read my stories.

From Sally, a fifth-grade teacher:

> I used to always BE IN CHARGE
> But now I know that kids can take ownership of their
> own learning.

I asked my undergraduates as part of their midsemester self-evaluation to reflect on the assumptions they had at the beginning of the year and where they are now, and to write an "I used to...but now." These future teachers write:

> I used to think that the only way to teach reading was through a structured program, But now I know that teachers aren't actors readingtheir lines from the basal reader script.
>
> *Pam*

> I used to think whole language was just reading aloud to my class every day,
> But now I know it is an entire philosophy and attitude about child-centered curriculum.
>
> *Becky*

> I used to think students should sit in their seats and do their work with no talking,
> Now I know that literacy is social, and they must gain experiences from one another.
>
> *Karen*

> I used to see no connection between reading and writing,
> But now I know they are nourished and supported by each other.
>
> *Susan*

> I used to dread dividing my class into ability groups,
> But now I know I'll never do that to kids.
>
> *Donna*

> I used to think I'd be stuck with basals and worksheets,
> But now I have thousands of stories and books to choose from.
>
> *Brenda*

> I used to think evaluation meant MMAT or the ITBS,
> But now I know that evaluation means self-evaluation as well as kid watching.
>
> *Sally*

OUR CHRYSALIS DIARY CONTINUES

WE ARE NOT THE SAME BEINGS WHO STARTED THIS DIARY. WE HAVE GROWN
WITH THE HELP OF CHILDREN, PARENTS, AND COLLEAGUES.

DOROTHY: We have gained outer knowledge that informs us and inner wisdom that sustains us.

KITTYE: We have grown,

DOROTHY: but just as important, our students have grown—many times, far beyond us.

KITTYE: We still have fears,

DOROTHY: but we know how to confront them

TOGETHER.

KITTYE: We continue to have problems. New ones replace the old ones.

DOROTHY: And the new ones are often more complex, demanding

AND EXCITING!

November 20, 1989:

KITTYE: This day of whole language

DOROTHY: points us toward literature and research and more study. This day of whole language

KITTYE: points us toward this summer when in August we meet in St. Louis for our first Whole Language Umbrella Conference. This day of whole language

DOROTHY: points us toward self-evaluation and reflection on what we believe and accept as good teaching and learning. This day of whole language

KITTYE: points us toward all the beauty and knowledge that can come to life in our classrooms.

Kittye Copeland and Dorothy Watson are faculty members at the University of Missouri, Columbia.

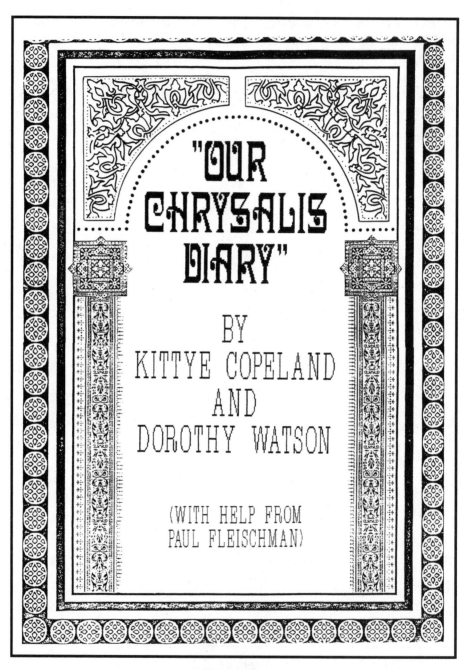

"OUR CHRYSALIS DIARY"

BY
KITTYE COPELAND
AND
DOROTHY WATSON

(WITH HELP FROM
PAUL FLEISCHMAN)

FIGURE 1

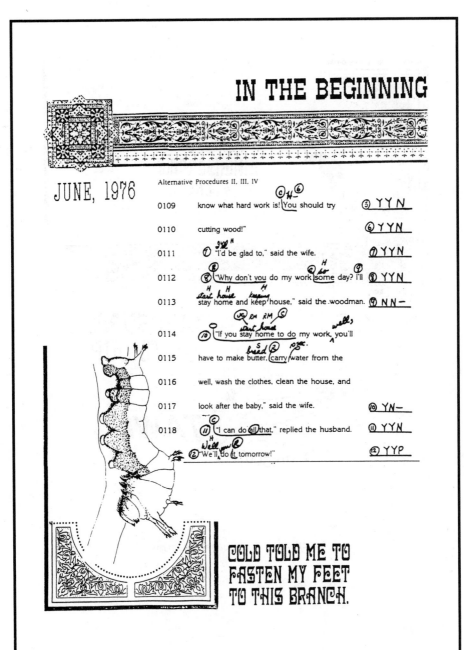

IN THE BEGINNING

JUNE, 1976

Alternative Procedures II, III, IV

0109	know what hard work is! You should try	⑤ Y Y N
0110	cutting wood!"	⑥ Y Y N
0111	⑦ "I'd be glad to," said the wife.	⑦ Y Y N
0112	⑧ "Why don't you do my work some day? I'll	⑧ Y Y N
0113	stay home and keep house," said the woodman.	⑨ N N —
0114	⑩ "If you stay home to do my work, you'll	
0115	have to make butter, carry water from the	
0116	well, wash the clothes, clean the house, and	
0117	look after the baby," said the wife.	⑩ Y N —
0118	⑪ "I can do all that," replied the husband.	⑪ Y Y N
	⑫ "We'll do it tomorrow!"	⑫ Y Y P

COLD TOLD ME TO FASTEN MY FEET TO THIS BRANCH.

FIGURE 2

I FEEL
IMMEASURABLY
ALONE.

SEPTEMBER, 1977

OUR SUPPORT
GROUP

TAWL

dedicated to language and learning

FIGURE 3

...AND PUNISHMENT

OCTOBER, 1982

Is it read or rēd?

Kittye Copeland, first-grade teacher at Ashland's elementary school, uses the "whole-language reading method" with Tanya Nilges left, Roxanne Gilmore and Heather Hamilton.

N. John Martini

Ashland teacher's new method spells controversy

By Brent Franzel
Missourian staff writer

guage approach is used.

HAVE ANY OTHERS
OF MY KIND
SURVIVED THIS
CATACLYSM?

FIGURE 4

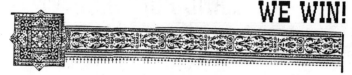

WE WIN!

NOVEMBER, 1982

Whole-language teaching approach used successfully in other areas

By Brent Franzel
Missourian staff writer

Reading method accepted in Columbia

The whole-language approach is not unique to Ashland. Many reading teachers in Columbia public schools use it. But Columbia parents seem satisified with its effectiveness.

"Not only has it not been a problem," says Board of Education member Patsy Garner, "it has been very successful."

active members. She believes there are other area teachers using the method who are not TAWL members.

"TAWL groups usually emerge from a university setting and spread to the surrounding area," Ms. Bixby explains.

But not all reading professionals

Americans were becoming functional illiterates as a result of innovative approaches to teaching. Phonetics is the best way to teach reading, he proclaimed.

He followed up his landmark treatise with an I-told-you-so article published in Family Circle magazine

Parents flock to support whole-language program

By Brent Franzel
Missourian staff writer

ASHLAND — About 100 parents — most in support of the whole-language approach used to teach reading at Southern Boone County R-1 Elementary School — flocked to a Wednesday night meeting. The meeting was held in response to parents' charges that the method makes children lazy, poor spellers and creates lax discipline in the classroom.

The method differs from traditional phonics, which begins with sounds

earn as much applause as that of supporters. Parent Jim Beasley, raising his voice above that applause, said, "We are very proud of Ms. (Kittye) Copeland's participation."

Although other teachers in the district use the approach, the controversy has centered on Ms. Copeland because of her vocal backing of the program.

Earlier this year, she was named outstanding teacher in content area by the International Reading Association. Her use of the revolutionary teaching method was an important

A BREEZE FROM THE SOUTH..

A FAINT GLIMPSE OF GREEN...

FIGURE 5

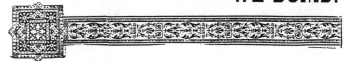

WE BOMB!

JULY, 1983

Please give us your impressions of this whole language
conference:

Dorothy Watson and
Kittye Copeland
need lobotomies !

FIGURE 6

FEBRUARY, 1989

WHOLE LANGUAGE umbrella

WINGS ARE GROWING.

FIGURE 7

Dear Ms. Copeland,
I think I sort of like dark
days although the baby dies.
Why did beth go when it was JO's
turn. I would've made her do it!
I think Beth doesn't like to fight with Jo
Is this book a true story? Why
I don't think so
did Amy get so upset about going
to her grandmothers house. I mean
she never has to talk to her just
explore.?
Kate
I think she is old and bossy

FIGURE 8

Dear Ms. Copeland,
You have of course answered
Was n't it an Aunt?
correctly. When I said explore I
ment she would explore her Aunt's
house. I thought that thier Aunt was
there grandmother, for she acted like
it. And I thought for sure that this was
a true story.
Kate

FIGURE 9

3. **What are the reasons we write?**

Eric:

So   Wen   we   goow
uP   We   will   Rnow
How   to   WRi te and
So   When   You   rite
Yeuso

FIGURE 10

Lara:
We write because we get to chose what
we wont, because we can shere what kend of
subject we wad likes to leun, for expeience
to commencate.

4. **Who do you write for?**

Lara   I write different stores for different
people.

Eric   I   right   to   mrs   copled

FIGURE 11

what makes a good writer?

6. spelg   rely   hard   and
Eric   sonthly   cut   the   wors
and   reniving   your   spling
words

6. Descriptive, good plot, not a dumb title or they
Lara   wont want to read it.

7. *who do you know is a good writer?*
   I Know Katie is a good writer because she
Lara   always makes it exiting, funny ect.

7.   *so* Evan   Dally   He   gets
Eric   He   Wrights   velly   net

FIGURE 12

CASEY O RILEY

Casey O' Riley was the best baseball player that ever played the
game. He could smack the ball so hard people said his ball
went up to 1007 miles perhour but he died in 1876 and every
wonce in a while hes ghost would aopear on Rigley feld in
chicago. Well I still remember when Casey O' Riley appeared on
Rigley Field in 1953 CUBS vs YANKEES BASEBALL GAME. It was the
bottem of the 5 Mickey Mantel was up, Stalard pitching and
before he started to pitch Casey O' Riley appeard on third
base.He took the bat and hit 5 people some in
  the stomach some in the head and then juist disappeared
in thin air and they still coald the inuasion of
Caasey O' Riley . I relly remembear in 1933 CUBS vs
THE S.T. LOUS Cardinals in Chicago wen Stan Muiaal
was going back and KACE O RILY apeard in the craoud
and hit 76 peopel and then disappeared
            THE END

                                    Eric

FIGURE 13

Paging Dr. McLaughlin floor 3, Dr. McLaughlin. If you will please
excuse me Mr. Flake I'm being paged on floor 3 said Dr. McLaughlin
now continue taking your Emycin and I will be in in 2 weeks. I
have a plane leaving tonight for Egypt and Dr. Stoltz will be
coming in tomorrow to check on you. Egypt! said Mr. Flake why on
earth are you going to Egypt? Well there have been people
reported to the Hospital because they have poor eating diets and
some of the (poor) people probably have never gone to the Doctor
and are very ill. Paging Dr. McLaughlin, Dr. McLaughlin floor 3,
room 101. Well, remember Dr. Stoltz will be coming in tomorrow to
check on you. I'll see you in a couple weeks said Dr. McLaughlin,
good bye said Mr. Fake and Mr. McLaughlin walked out the door and
into the elevator. (But we have to get one thing straight hear
Dr. McLaughlin's first name is John, so in some of the story I
will be referring to him as John.)

Once John reached floor 3 and was in room 101, he saw that he had
a new patient to tend to. "Well my name is Dr. McLaughlin and I
will be your Doctor for about "Oh" 1 day said John, 1 day why only
1 day? said the patient, well I'm going on a trip tonight and will
not be back for a couple of weeks, so I think maybe since I'll
only be here today that you will probably want to have a new
Doctor, so I'll get you one and he could probably be in in about
30 or 45 minutes. Okay answered the patient and Dr. McLaughlin
left h room and took a elevator to the parking garage where his
car was parked.

After John returned home he immediately started packing more of
his clothes into his suit case. John, Yes Terry (Terry was Johns
wife's name. Terry short for Therese). John and Terry were both in
their 50s and 60s and were old enough to have kids, they do have 3
kids, John the 2nd the oldest, then came Carolyn then Jane Ellen
and they are all old enough to have kids too. John has 2 kids
(short for John the 3rd and Leah then Carolyn's kid Lara (a
wonderful child) then Jane Ellen's kid Baby Gerath.) John! asked
Terry, yes he answered, all your shorts and your short sleeved
shirts are in your dresser drawer, believe me you will definitely
want them.

Just as soon as 5:30 creeped up John and Terry were about ready to
head to the Detroit airport and get ready for the long, long trip
to Egypt.

TO BE CONTINUED

By Lara Birkes

FIGURE 14

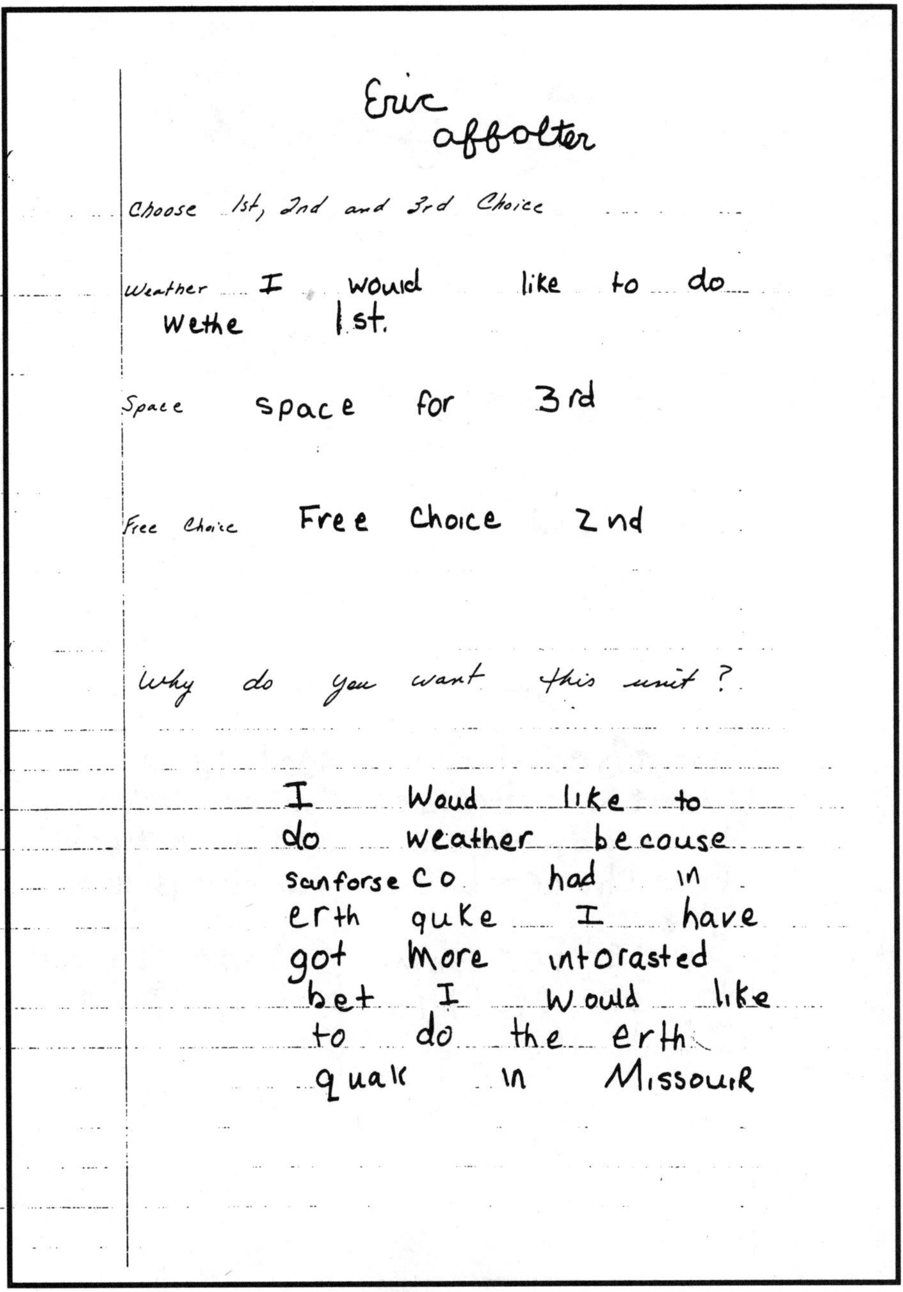

Eric
affolter

Choose 1st, 2nd and 3rd Choice

Weather   I   would   like   to   do
Wethe   1st.

Space   space   for   3rd

Free Choice   Free Choice   2nd

Why do you want this unit?

I   Woud   like   to
do   weather   becouse
sanforse Co   had   in
erth   quke   I   have
got   More   intorasted
bet   I   would   like
to   do   the   erth
quak   in   Missouir

FIGURE 15

Jack

Jack

Choose 1st, 2nd and 3rd Choice

Weather **1st**

Space **3rd**

Free Choice **2nd**

Why do you want this unit?

Weather – It's good to study Weather. Besides, we may even get to study the earthquakes in Missouri.

Free Choice– Large Variety is what I like.

Space– For some reason I'm not to fond of this but if I haft I'll do it.

FIGURE 16

Barberfish

* Makes Profession of eating small Parasites off of fish!
* Lives entirely free-to-do-Anything.
* Performs Dance in front of other fishes nose
* Feeds on Parosites
* Discovered one day that Other fish suffer from Ectoparasites whom Suck Blood.
* It was so Successful, That now In the care of Other fish
* Positions on cortain place when has nothing to Do.
* After Dance, Other fish finds Posture.
* Lives in Western Pacific and Indian Oceans.
* Performs all day long.
* Lives in Warmer waters.
*

FIGURE 17

BARBER FISH AND THE DEAD SEA
STARTING OFF
When you think about the name "Barber Fish", what do you think?
That's a pretty stupid name, right? But when you consider the
things the "Barber Fish" has done, maybe you'll change your mind.
No? Well, O.K., i'll tell you a little bit. But this is your last
chance to change your mind. AHEM...... "Barber Fish" have an
interesting profession, it grooms other fish of their disgusting
ecto-parasites! The parasites, stick themselves to other fish,
intending to suck blood. The Barber Fish discovered it's fellow
fishes problems and set out to eat the nasty parasites. In fact,
it was so succesful that the Barber Fish is now primarily used in
cleaning Tropical fish. DANCE PARTY,USA
The barber fish lives in the warmer waters of the pacific
ocean(hey, all you disco fans out there. The barber fish does a
little 'dance', before the larger fish's nose. Then the other
fish, thus happy with a nearby cleaning service, finds a posture.
For the little fish to clean the bigger fish, the bigger fish may
even open up it's gills!).   DEJA VU,BARBER FISH
The barber fishperforms this silly dance all day long. This fish
lives intirely independant. If it can't find 'business', it will
find a different place to 'work'.
5-MINUTE BREAK
Well,now. We learned a lot, didn't we? Good. Now let me tell you a
little bit about the Dead sea. No? Your mind is full? Aw c'mon,
just a little bit more!
HERE WE GO AGAIN!
The dead sea is the saltiest lake in the world. It is near the
country's Israel and Jordan. The surface is 1'300 feet below sea
level. The waters are supplied by the Jordan river.
THE NAMES THE GAME
You can probably guess why this sea is called the 'dead sea'. All
the fish are dead. The greeks originated the name 'dead sea'.
During the millions of years since the dead sea was originated, it
has had such names as the Offensive sea, Eastern sea, Asphaltic
sea, Sea of Araba, Sea of lot, and(this is my favorite) The sea.
THE SEA OF THE BIBLE
In the bible, there is a recounted article about the catastraphic
earthquake that hit in the Abraham time. The bible accounts of
just about everything in the dead seas long history.
YUCK!SALT!INFO!(info?)
On the surface of the dead sea, there is 227 to 275 grains
of salt(WOW!). The salt contains calcium, potassium, sodium,
bromide,and sulfate. Ever since 1930, some salt has been used
for gasoline and fertilizer. Potassium and bromide are the most
valuable salts.
BOOK IT!
Ever since 1947, a collection of dead sea scrolls have been found.
The story is simple: a little boy was looking for his lost lamb
and found the scrolls inside a cave. These are the following
scrolls found:(1)2 copies of the book of Isaiah.(2)A manuel of
discipline.(3)The book of hynms.(4)Final war manuel.(5)Habakhuk
book-2 chapters.(6)Genesis paraphrase.
THE FACTS I FORGOT
Oh my gosh, your brain is overloading! Just a little bit more! On
the north side of the dead sea, the salt comes from evaporation.
The scrolls are found in Qumran. From 1880-1935 the dead sea
slowly grew. Today its shrink-KABOOM!

FIGURE 18

THE DADZY NYMS
HAS MA

Aaron

Sea Otters

They Mosle Sam On Theer
Bas. They Slep And Eat on Theer
Bus they Can S nder Water
For 3 Mns.

Chandler

FIGURE 19

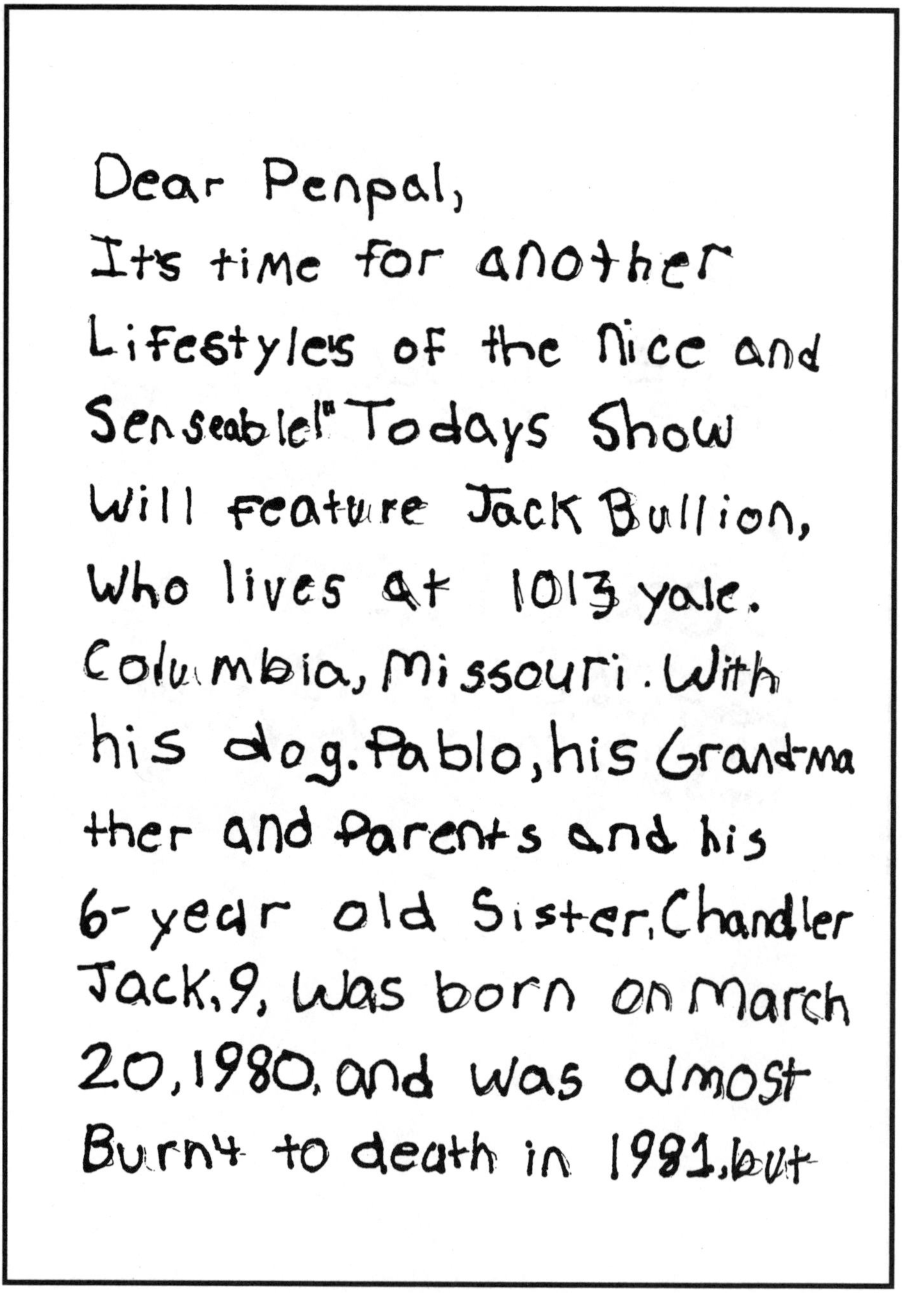

Dear Penpal,
Its time for another Lifestyles of the Nice and Senseable" Todays Show will feature Jack Bullion, Who lives at 1013 yale. Columbia, Missouri. With his dog. Pablo, his Grandmother and Parents and his 6-year old Sister, Chandler Jack, 9, was born on March 20, 1980, and was almost Burnt to death in 1981, but

FIGURE 20

Jack ~~yuck~~

recovered quickly. He now finds pastimes in watching sports and studying. He wants to be a biologist and/or a football playe

Questions:
How old are you?
Are you a Boy/Girl?
What's your favorite food?
What do you want to be when you grow up?

FIGURE 21

STULL WINS DEBUT

BY SPORTS EDITOR
Jack W. Bullion

Many people thought that Bob Stull who virtually turned around the football
programs at the University of Massachusetts and UTEP (University of Texas
at ElPaso) was hoping to make a impact on the game Saturday vs. TCU (Texas
Christian University). Even though a defensive battle, the start looked like
TCU all the way. The horned frogs struck quickly. With 1 yard touchdown
run. Missouri got the ball, and either the Missouri offense was just warming
up or TCU's defense was playing GOOD. Missouri punted the ball and TCU
got it back. TCU was mounting a good drive until the Missouri defense stiffened,
and TCU had to settle for a field goal. But wait! Missouri blocked it!
Missouri had the ball but could not convert. TCU had the ball back, but had to
settle for another field goal try. But it was blocked and returned for good
field position. This time, MU scored a touchdown. TCU kicked a field goal
just before the half to lead 10 - 7. The third quarter was Defensive Battle.
In the fourth quarter MU scored and TCU failed to cover. In the end, I think
it was MU's late game defense that stopped TCU.

By Jack

FIGURE 22

FRANCESCO PETRARCH
(1304-1374)
Francesco Petrarch was born on July 20,1304,and later became an
Italian Poet, Founder of Humanism and Man of Letters. His Father
was exiled from Florence, Italy, shortly before Francesco was
born. Born in Arezzo, Italy, he lived in Tuscany, Italy, until he
was 8. His father found a job in Avignon, Italy, as a notary in
the Papel Court. So the family moved to Avignon. When he was 12,
he went to study law at Montpieller and Bologna. Shortly after his
father's death in 1326, he moved back to Avignon. On Good Friday,
1327, he met"Laura". He often punned her name on"Laurel"(A symbol
of Poetic Achievement). In 1330, he recieved the Tonsure, which
enabled him to hold beneficial service's for the church. In 1337,
he moved to Vaucluse, a valley near Avignon, and even though he
traveled very much, he still considered this his home. He had two
ambitions in life: The love of Fame and The love of Women. Even
though "Laura"died in 1348 of the Black Death, his heart was still
with her. The love of Fame grew less as he grew older but the love of
Women increased. He described love as "Pleasing Pains". His poetry
skills increased after "Laura" died. And although he never
married,he had two children named Giovvani and Francesca. He
expressed his and Laura's feelings in his poems. He also did latin
works in 600 letters. His works have been admired all over Europe
and they earned the name "Petrarchism". In fact, even Shakespeare
used Petrarchism! Petrarch was also fond of Oxymoron the mixture
of two things together that are opposed and if read carefully by
the reader, can be understood. He put Greek literature back in
motion. He got tired of public life and moved to Arqua, Italy,and
died on the night of July 18-19, 1374.

β' κ₁₃ ‾ ₁⁓₄ ξ,₃,⁓ς₁'

FIGURE 23

P.J.'s Travels

In the small World of an Ant the only enemy that all fear is a Size 15 Reebok.

Another Potential enemy of the ant is a Nike Air coming down like an Atomic Bomb. But P.J. ~~skinnylegs~~ skinnylegs never feared those things. A daring little Ant. P.J. had just come home from Driving MatchBox cars. "Hi Mom!"

FIGURE 24

STUDENT SURVEY SHEET
(LITERATURE GROUPS)

Name: *Gary*   Date: *Nov. 13, 1989*

Rating Scale: 3=Great Job!
              2=Pretty good!
              1=I could do better!
              0=I blew it--I'll do better next time!

SPEAKING

1 1. I speak clearly and loudly enough for all group members to hear me--not just the teacher.

1 2. I add my fair share to the discussion; not too much, not too little.

2 3. I stay on the subject.

3 4. I don't interrupt when someone else is speaking.

1 5. I look at everyone while I'm speaking, not just the teacher.

LISTENING

3 1. I listen to other members of the group.

3 2. I look at the person speaking.

2 3. I encourage others to speak.

1 4. I ask questions when I don't understand what someone else is talking about.

READING/DISCUSSING

2 1. As I read the story, I understood it.

   I was prepared for the discussion by:

1 2. Reading the assigned pages.

0 3. Writing in my literature journal.

2 4. Thinking about what I would say in the group.

1 5. I related the story to things that have happened to me.

1 6. I compared this book to others I've read.

FIGURE 25

The discussion was good today because: Evrybody (was Caught up (besides Gary Who didn't write his reactions but read the whole book)

We could have had a better discussion if we would have Had Gary Write his reactions

The discussion was good today because: We all had reacsons exsept Gary

We could have had a better discussion if Gary had reacsons

The discussion was good today because: We got to hear everybody's reackhons. And we talked about the storyes.

We could have had a better discussion if we would have Better reactions and Better storys.

FIGURE 26

The discussion was good today because: *We got to hear everybody's reackhens. and we talked about the storyes.*

We could have had a better discussion if we would have *Better reactions and Better storys.*

Adapted by Delores Welshmeyer for Grade Four Reading Discussion Groups, from D.J. Watson's "Assessment Suggestions for Literature Discussion Groups" in Ideas and Insights: Language Arts in the Elementary School, NCTE, 1987.

FIGURE 27

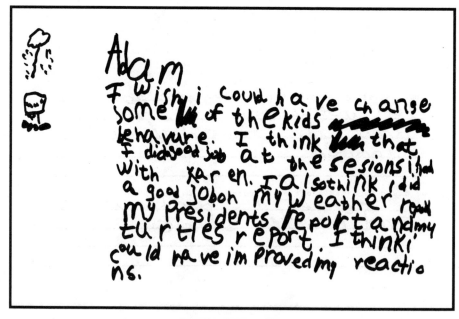

FIGURE 28

Perspective From a TAWL Teacher

In undergoing metamorphosis to whole language, we learn much from our colleagues who are also struggling with the confrontations and challenges at the chalk face. The sense of community that exists among whole language teachers and learners is one of the most unique and satisfying aspects of this movement. Where whole language teachers are gathered, there is constant engagement, discussion, sharing, and debate about what they do in their classrooms and why they do it. Visit these classrooms with me and experience these days of whole language.

JEAN FENNACY, DEBORAH MANNING,
AND VALERIE PORTER

A Year of Pen-Pal Letters

AUTHENTICITY IN LITERACY EDUCATION

As the 1988-89 school year approached, three educators, a second-grade teacher, an eighth-grade English/history teacher, and a college professor in teacher education were looking forward to the opening of school with great anticipation. Their minds were filled with classroom scenes of students actively engaged in purposeful learning. All three were planning experiences to engage their pupils in reading and writing as tools of learning. As a common element, each one was planning to include a writers' workshop where students, both young and old, would find stimulation and satisfaction in drafting, sharing, revising, and, on occasion, publishing personal pieces.

By the end of the first week of school, however, the second- and eighth-grade teachers were doubting the wisdom of their plans and, more serious, by the end of the first month, questioning their ability to teach.

These veteran teachers, who were recognized as knowledgeable and successful practitioners of whole language theory, each faced classes of students with far more than the normal share of troubled youngsters whose behavior in the classroom and on the school grounds left much to be desired.

In these two particular settings, the writers' workshops the teachers had so carefully planned never quite got off the ground. Yet, not only did writing eventually flourish in their classrooms, but it became a critical factor as a means by which the students found their voices and reached out beyond themselves to others. Quite by accident, it was the writing of pen-pal letters that linked these classes and stimulated authentic authorship. This paper documents the story of these classrooms, first from the college instructor's viewpoint, next in the words of the second-grade teacher, and finally from the perspective of the eighth-grade teacher.

THE TEACHER EDUCATOR

At the beginning of the school year, I was interested in having my teacher-education students learn more about young children's literacy development firsthand. I asked Debbie Manning if my students could write to her second-graders for the course of the fall semester. She eagerly agreed, and my college students initiated the exchange the first week of school. As a class we brainstormed what we might write about. At the beginning of the semester, we took class time to write letters, but as the term progressed, letter writing became part of the students' homework.

The future teachers eagerly looked forward to the weekly exchange of letters. When I handed out the letters, we spent considerable class time reading, sharing, and commenting on the pen pals' news. Since I was a frequent visitor to the second-grade classroom, I was able to report on some of the recent important happenings, such as the field trip to a fire station or a special classroom visitor. This information often helped us decipher the children's writing. I found that in much the same way that the second-graders needed support in reading the adults' letters, the adults needed support in reading the youngsters' letters. In fact, it was as normal for me to say "Try to read what your pen pal wrote first and help each other, then I'll be around to assist you if you can't figure out the writing" as it was for Debbie to say the same thing to her second-graders.

As the semester wore on, the college students became quite proficient in reading the youngsters' letters and took great delight in their writing development, a skill I believed would prove invaluable once they had classrooms of their own. I also was pleased to see my students focus on the letters' contents rather than seeing errors in convention. This seems to be a critical aspect in training teachers new to whole language.

The activity turned out to be so successful that Debbie wanted her students to continue letter writing in the spring. Recognizing that the college students would be busy in student teaching assignments and most likely would not be able to continue writing on a regular basis, we sought a new source for the pen pals. Valerie Porter, a mutual friend, accepted the invitation, and during the spring semester the second-graders and Val's eighth-graders corresponded weekly.

Studying exchanges of letters helped us view this pen-pal experience as a graphic example of language learning through meaningful and functional use within the school context. At the heart of whole language theory is the understanding that language, both oral and written, develops through real, genuine use. Reading and writing as well as speaking are learned not as abstract systems to be applied later to various uses. Rather, children learn language and its purposes simultaneously when they are admitted into the club of fellow language users. As Frank Smith suggests, "Children learn to read and write effectively only if they are admitted into a community of written-language users" (1988). We have come to a personal appreciation for the meaning of those words and are all the more committed to filling our classrooms with authentic, real-world literacy experiences for our students.

Over the course of the second year, we saw tremendous growth not only in terms of quantity, but also in quality of writing. By focusing on meaning rather than convention, the students were encouraged to take risks and write as best they could and about what was meaningful to them. In doing so, the children discovered, as Wells suggests (1986), that they had experiences to share, stories to tell that others found interesting. Indeed, they belonged to the fraternity of writers. They grew as writers and their writing became more and more conventional. They discovered their best efforts would be celebrated. Mistakes were natural, not something to be feared. As second-grader Gregory G. wrote to his eighth-grade pen pal Sean:

Dear Sean,
ts OK you mist speld my name every body makes
mistak-es even I do.

The freedom to write as best they could allowed the children to take risks with language and, as a result, gradually develop as more and more proficient language users. The students' letters were never edited by the teachers, yet growth in convention was evident. Two of Andrew's letters illustrate this development.

In September Andrew's letter to Diane looked like this:

Yes i feed my anomos avre day is your work hrd my work is a lidllbet hard. intell then Godby Anderw

In this letter written during the second week of school, Andrew used 21 words, 57 percent of which were conventionally spelled. He used one period at the end of the body of the letter, but did not use other punctuation to separate his sentences. There was no greeting to Diane, but he did answer a question she asked him about feeding his animals. He extended a question to her.

By early May, Andrew was corresponding weekly to eighth-grader Jess, and one of his letters looked like this:

Dear Jess,
Stop! calling me Andy. I do not like the name that you call me. Our wale dose not live in our classroom. it lives in the sea. It is a Boy. Funny name for a boy ha? do you leke bakesitball? it is a good sport ha?

Here, Andrew used 64 words, 82 percent of which were correctly spelled. Not only did his letters get longer and his spelling improve, the form of his letters became far more conventional. He learned to separate the greeting and his signature from the body of the letter. He even indented as he began the body. His use of ending punctuation became largely conventional. Yet he never took a spelling test, did a punctuation worksheet, or experienced a formal lesson on letter writing.

He addressed several distinct topics, including an answer to his pen pal's question about an adopted whale. He also asked two questions of his own. He demonstrated his understanding of how the text of letters are produced, and even though he did not physically show his paragraphs, he organized his letter into four chunks of ideas. Andrew's development as a writer supports the notion that the genre of the letter is the foundation for the essay. As Graves states: "A careful examination of children's ability to state opinions, express contrary points of view, or write letters filled with information will provide evidence that they are ready to work with the essay long before it is introduced in most school curricula. Children have so little opportunity to write meaningful nonfiction that we seldom find out what they're doing in the nonfiction genre." (Graves, 1989, p. 53)

By using letter writing as an integral part of the classroom events and by reaching out to others through letters, the students discovered the letter as a genre could serve their own needs. They filled them with information that was personally meaningful to them and, in the process, showed us how capable they were.

As we began to ponder what it was that made the pen-pal letter exchange such a success in our classrooms, we realized that the crucial elements of time, choice, and response that Hansen (1987) reminds us are essential for meaningful writing to occur were all present. Priority time was set aside weekly for letter writing. When the letters were delivered, little else could have been accomplished anyway, for the students were eager to read them and respond immediately. This was as true at the college level as it was in the second- and eighth-grade classrooms. The degree of interest was great, and another planned curricular activity ran second best at that moment. Perhaps second-grader Mai expressed this feeling best when she wrote to her pen pal Krysti:

> Dear Krysti, I am very glad your pen pal letters came to our room because we keep on saying to our teacher, "Where are the pen pal letters?"

In addition to time, choice was an integral aspect of the pen-pal experience. Students themselves chose what they would write about. At the very beginning, we held class discussions addressing possible topics of interest, but the choices remained in the students' hands. The range of those topics was remarkable.

Finally, return letters provided the much-needed feedback or response that writers in particular and language learners in general need to ever refine their language craft. Writing alone does not produce better writers. But when writers get response to their ideas, and when that response comes frequently and regularly from people with whom they have developed a caring relationship, the possibility for growth seems endless.

THE SECOND-GRADE TEACHER

We've heard and read many times over that children learn to read by reading and to write by writing, but never in our wildest dreams did we anticipate such powerfully authentic writing to happen in school.

Both second- and eighth-grade classes had ethnically diverse mixtures of children with such low self-esteem that getting from point A to point B was a major task at the beginning of the school year. These children desperately needed someone to really care and to honestly respond to their needs and ideas.

As we examined the letter exchanges between pen pals, we discovered a wide range of topics. Not surprisingly, some of the first categories we found were sports, family, and pets. These exchanges were rather superficial and identical in context, almost on a par with Dick, Jane, and Spot. On the other hand, books and boyfriends and girlfriends are examples of topics that began to take on more authentic qualities. These exchanges lasted over extended periods of time and were unique to each writer.

But what we did not anticipate were the in-depth grand conversations that only come about when an author takes ownership of his or her own writing and really and truly cares. The sharing of feelings, worries, fears, and concerns with a genuine reaching out in support of each other are some examples of categories of topics the students wrote about that have left an indelible imprint on all of us.

When two people meet for the first time, generally conversations are based on familiar topics in hopes that some common ground can be established. In this way, the dialogue can continue and new interests can be explored. We found this to be true with the pen-pal letters. The students wrote about themselves and their families rather frequently during the first few exchanges.

The sharing of school experiences was common in most letters throughout the school year. Second-grader Teresa wrote to Jody, her eighth-grade pen pal, the following:

> We're dissecting frogs, starfish, worms and black grasshoppers. I think I'm dissecting a frog. I don't know and I hope I dissect a frog because I think a frog will be more interesting for me— but it's going to be disgusting— I mean touching gross. I wonder what it looks like in the first place.

Meghan, also a second-grader, wrote to her pen pal the following:

We have not done our CAT testing yet. We are going to
have our CAT test in two weeks. At least we get snacks.
Meghan to Jarred (eighth grade)

Sports was another favorite topic among many of the students. Matt
and Greg carried on the following correspondence:

Do you like football? I do. My favorite team is the 49ers.
I was glad they won the Super Bowl. Jerry Rice is my
favorite player. I enjoy watching other sports too. My
favorite basketball team is the Lakers and my favorite
baseball team is the Mets. I don't know if I liked sports
in 2nd grade. Do you?
Matt (eighth grade) to Greg (second grade)

Greg responded:

Yes, I like football and my favorite team is the 49ers too!
I like sports in 2nd grade.

Greg to Matt

Talk about hobbies and pets seemed to fill the other rather awkward
gaps in the initial letter exchanges. Robby, an eighth-grader, expressed
concern to his pen pal about having something in common:

Some of my hobbies are collecting football cards and
baseball cards. I also like riding my motorcycle. I hope
we will have something in common.
Robby to Thomas (second grade)

Thomas replied:

I collect baseball cards too! I have some football cards.
So we do have something in common.
Thomas to Robby

Since reading and writing go hand in hand, it did not take the students long before they shared a common love for literature. Discussions of literature studies, book talks, authors, and illustrators filled many letters time and time again. Mai's letter to her pen pal Krysti is very informative:

> I went to see Byrd Baylor on Thursday. Byrd Baylor said she picks her own illustrators for her books. Do you know Byrd Baylor? Byrd Baylor is a writer and she is 63 years old. She lives in the desert with a dead walnut tree in her house. And my class gave Byrd Baylor new walnut tree to replace her old one.
>
> *Mai (second grade) to Krysti (eighth grade)*

Correspondence between Gregory, a second-grader, and Sean, an eighth-grader, show the respect the children demonstrated for each other's opinions.

> Do you know what lit studies are?
>
> *Gregory to Sean*

> I am in a lit studies group so I know what one is. It is pretty fun because you learn about things.
>
> *Sean to Gregory*

Later in the correspondence Gregory asked:

> Have you read the book Jackie Robinson Bravest Man in Baseball? I like baseball.
>
> *Gregory to Sean*

Sean replied:

> I haven't read that book but I will look for it and read it. It is probably a good book if you liked it.
>
> *Sean to Gregory*

Another topic that seemed to be of great interest related to boy-friend/girlfriend situations. Many a heart-throbbing story unfolded, and I wouldn't be surprised to see a few of them in print someday. Erika, a second-grader, and Pepper, an eighth-grader, shared the following exchange:

I have a boyfriend and his name is Thomas and Ryan.
They are in my classroom and they both like me too.
Erika to Pepper

How long have you liked Thomas and Ryan? Are they
cute? How old are you? How old are they? I have a
boyfriend. His name is Jake. He goes to Bass Lake.
Pepper to Erika

I did not know you had a boyfriend. Me and Thomas
and Ryan were together on the first day of school but
Thomas did not like me for a girlfriend at all. Now he
likes me. Pepper, Thomas and Ryan are cute. Is your
boyfriend cute? I am 9 years old. Ryan is 7 and Thomas
is 8. How old are you?
Erika to Pepper

Once relationships had been established between pen pals, small
tokens of friendship were exchanged such as photos and cards, drawings,
friendship bracelets, and various treasured bones that had been extracted
from owl pellets during science. Shannon wrote to Alana:

Thanks for the skull. That was thoughtful of you. I put
it on my dresser. Well, thanks again for the skull.
Maybe someday I'll give you something in return.
Shannon (eighth grade) to Alana (second grade)

Elizabeth wrote to Jubilene:

Next time I will give you a picture of me. I will give you
a friendship bracelet too! Oh and thank you for the
Valentine card that you gave me and I like you and
thank you for writing to me.
Elizabeth (second grade) to Jubilene (eighth grade)

I really do want a picture of you. Thanks for the friendship bracelet. It was really neat. I made a friendship
bracelet for you too. I hope you like it. Thank you for
liking me and you're welcome for me writing to you.
Jubilene to Elizabeth

Addresses and phone numbers were also exchanged. There seemed to be authentic reasons to continue to write after school ended. Pepper initiated the conversation with her second-grade pen pal, Erika:

> Do you want to write each other over the summer? If you do here's my address Can you give me yours? I would really love to hear from you when school's out. I am glad I got the chance to be your pen pal. I will miss your letters if you don't write to me over the summer. Your letters are very fun to read.
>
> *Pepper to Erika*

Pepper and Erika did indeed exchange letters over the summer, and so did several other students. Pepper closed her letters to Erika with "Erika and Pepper: Friends forever."

Often, one pen pal or the other needed clarification or more information to make sense of what had been said. Thomas's letter to eighth-grader Robby is an example of this type of correspondence:

> What's "got to jet" mean? You wrote that at the end off your last letter.
>
> *Thomas to Robby*

> "Got to jet" means I have to go like leave. I thought you would know that but I guess you didn't.
>
> *Robby to Thomas*

As students began to take more and more ownership of their letters, they were also willing to take more and more risks. Their self-esteem rose, and they felt worthy of imparting words of wisdom. Again, Thomas provides us with an example:

> Do you know what an owl pellet is? It's the stuff that an owl can't digest like bones and feet. We'll get to dissect one. In your letter you should find a thing of bones such as shoulder blades, hind legs and skull fragments.
>
> *Thomas to Robby*

In response, his pen pal told Thomas all about toothpaste:

I just finished a science project on which toothpaste works the best on stained teeth. I used real teeth that I have had pulled. I found out that Aquafresh is the best toothpaste you can buy.

Robby to Thomas

Second-grader Teresa provides us with another example:

Do you know who Donald H. Graves is? Well, I'm going to tell you what he says. In 10 minutes you write. You need a simple question. Then ask, "What struck you?"

Teresa to Jody (eighth grade)

Then the students really began to care. They each had a special person to share and confide in, someone they could trust. And as these friendships grew, so too did their letters—far beyond all expectations. Students began to confide in each other, as did Teresa in a letter to Jody:

Yesterday I was sick - boring. I had to be baby sat like a baby because there was nobody to take care of me. Nothing to do. I'm well today because I don't want to be treated like a baby.

Teresa to Jody

I hope you are feeling better. I know what it's like to be treated like a baby.

Jody to Teresa

In another letter to Jody, Teresa wrote:

Tomorrow I'm going to be with my mom 'cause my dad and mom don't live with my other mother anymore. But they are taking turns at every other month I get to be with my dad or mom.

Teresa to Jody

And Jody responded:

I'm sorry to hear about your parents. Who do you live with more or like you said that your parents trade off of having you for the month. It must be hard living at two different homes.

Jody to Teresa

There was also a special pride the students began to feel for each other. Notice Jason's message to Max:

I'm really proud that you're a winner in the Peach Blossom. Our class went to a Almond Blossom Festival and we won. We read a poem called "Meanwhile Back at the Ranch." I had a solo part in it and I did pretty good. All together our class got an Excellent.

Jason (eighth grade) to Max (second grade)

Students shared feelings, worries, and fears that needed to be addressed but so often get set aside for lack of a supportive audience. For example, when one of our second-grade students, Jaime, was hit by an automobile, eighth-grader Jubilene wrote to Elizabeth:

I really am sorry about what happened to Jaime. I will write her a letter. How did you feel after you heard about her accident? I felt really bad. After all the fun she probably had on the day of the picnic and then something bad happening.

Jubilene to Elizabeth

Letters even contained advice, and it seemed that no one was short-changed in this area. Notice the ongoing exchange on the topic:

Do you like writing and reading? I do. In fact I love it.

Max (second grade) to Jason

No, I don't like reading and writing but I am glad you do because it is good to like school, but I don't like school that much.

Jason to Max

Why aren't you good at reading and writing?
> *Max to Jason*

The reason I don't like reading and writing is because I'm not good at it but don't you stop liking it.
> *Jason to Max*

Then there was eighth-grader Sean who gave Gregory some job tips:

I got a job cleaning horse stalls and let me tell you it is not what it's cracked up to be. If you ever get a job, don't clean stalls because they really stink.
> *Sean to Gregory (second grade)*

The reaching out to, supporting, and caring for each other was evident in all of the pen-pal letters by the end of the year. Greg expressed his feelings this way:

I wanted to thank you for writing all those powerful letters that you wrote to me.
> *Greg (second grade) to Matt (eighth grade)*

And Jaime wrote to Mick:

I am sorry you did not do very good on your wrestling match. Even [if] you did not win, I still say you are a winner to me.
> *Jaime (second grade) to Mick (eighth grade)*

Notice, too, how Shannon reached out to share her fears and how Alana not only responds, but extends an invitation to continue the relationship they have over the summer.

I have 8 more days until school's out. [The] last day of school I go home and get ready for my graduation. I'm so nervous.
> *Shannon (eighth grade) to Alana (second grade)*

I wish you luck to graduate to high school. I hope you have fun in high school. Send me letters so you can still remember me. I'll put where I live and my phone number and, remember, call the operator first.

Alana to Shannon

Just as bulbs planted in the fall develop, take root, and, over time, flourish, the friendships found through letter writing grew and grew. Sometimes growing is a very silent thing. Sometimes we can't even tell growth is happening, but that doesn't mean it isn't. When children are allowed time, choice, and response in writing, when they are allowed to find their own voices and share their innermost thoughts with someone who genuinely shows interest and love, the flowers that blossom in their authorship as well as in their persons are uniquely beautiful with promises of future beauty to unfold.

THE EIGHTH-GRADE TEACHER

I was surprised at my class's enthusiasm for the pen-pal project. After all, they didn't agree on much, and many of the different factions were at odds. However, they acted like a family whenever their second-grade pen-pal letters arrived. Everything stopped. There was silence while the letters were distributed and read privately, then the letters *had* to be shared. Each student read aloud his/her letter, and we all pieced together and followed what was happening in Debbie's classroom. My students then sat down to write their replies.

Through their actions, my students told me that the pen-pal program was important. On one occasion, the letters arrived on a day we were scheduled to go to the high school for an orientation. Paul saw me bury the letters in my closet. I was absent from class the next day and returned to find that Paul had distributed the letters and was remorseless. In a subsequent class discussion, I learned that no one in the class could wait for the letters. They were *their* letters and they *had* to have them. No one worried about violating my closet or the instructions I had given the substitute. Paul didn't need to be forgiven; he was a hero!

I'll never forget Gabe's face the day I told him I had passed out all the second-graders' letters and no, there did not seem to be one for him. Gabe was a large boy, and I had to look up to see his eyes. There was an incredible look of sadness and hurt. I was taken aback; after all, Gabe had done little in school besides disrupting and tormenting some of the other boys. The effects of this pen-pal project were startling!

Deadlines were hectic, but not as bad with this group as you might imagine from their behavior. My students took pride in their letters and knew that their pen pals would be waiting. Moreover, I never found a pen-pal letter lying around. One boy, Mike, kept his letters in plastic page covers! They cared and demonstrated by trying to write clearly and descriptively, neatly, and in a conversational and friendly tone. My students sent pictures, photos, friendship bracelets, greeting cards, bookmarks, baseball cards, and stories. They wrote a personalized children's book for their pen pals. It was as if their "better half" were communicating.

What were the eighth-grade letters like? They had an authentic, friendly, caring "voice." They sought to make friends and to communicate. They asked questions about what they heard was happening in Debbie's class. My students shared incidents from our classroom and their lives. They gave advice and encouragement and even exchanged personal feelings. For my students, the pen-pal experience offered a way they could be positive and wonderful. They were. The best field trip we took was at the end of the year to meet Debbie's class. I didn't feel like Mrs. Gestapo. My point is this was a wonderfully loving experience for my hard-core, tough class. It was OK to be nice and sweet. They responded. The pen-pal program worked because it was real.

At the end of the year, I gave my class a Quick Write and a questionnaire about the pen-pal program. My eighth-graders reported that their pen-pal experience was extremely valuable and had had a significant effect on their writing and on their lives.

First, every one of my students enjoyed having a pen pal. They said, "I enjoyed it very much," "It was fun," "I met a lot of new people," "It was an exciting experience," "She taught me new things," "It made me feel special and needed." Many felt the pen-pal program had opened their cultural and ethnic horizons. A common quote was "We're all the same."

All of my students agreed that my future eighth-graders should have the same experience. Only one boy thought he would have preferred a pen pal of his own age.

I wanted to know how the pen-pal program could be made better. Five of my students said it was perfect, a surprising comment since little is ever judged perfect by an eighth-grader! Others wanted more visits, to start earlier in the year, and to have the second-graders visit us. One boy was even willing to raise money so that we could all go on a trip together to an amusement park.

Three of my eighth-graders noticed that their pen pal's writing had improved over the course of the exchange. One girl even said her pen pal's letters were exciting to read.

I asked my students if they liked writing letters. Their answer was an overwhelming yes. Nathan remarked, "The letters let me express my feelings about what happens in my environment and find out what is happening at Dailey School." Others said "I felt like I was talking to them," and, "I made a new friend" and "I love writing letters, and I love to receive them." Robby wrote, "It is a friend you never see, but hear."

In response to my query "How did exchanging letters affect your writing?" my students stated: "I wrote stories," "I wrote stories for kids and started writing about my first- and second- grade experiences," "I had to write in detail because if I didn't the second graders were always asking questions," "It made my writing better, it made me write longer letters, and letters to other people." Finally, Jubilene wrote, "It inspired me to do more pieces of writing."

I had never had a pen-pal program with my eighth-grade students before. Now, I wouldn't go a year without such a program; it is too valuable an experience. The authenticity of their writing carried over into the pieces they wrote for writing workshop, into the literature logs they kept for history, and into their dialogue journals, which they kept for reading—the three subjects I teach in my core class. My students became enthusiastic and caring writers. At the end of the year, Pepper wrote to me about the pen-pal program. Here is what she said:

> Mrs. Porter,
> I really loved writing to Erika. We found we had a lot in common. We both love sports and some of the same teams. She likes to read books and she loved my book for her. It made me feel the time it took to write and illustrate the children's book was worth it. She is really cute. It gave me the chance to get to know a person and build a friendship. She is black and I am white. It just goes to show white and black are the same. I hope she wants to write over the summer. I loved to get her letters and see how her writing got better each time. Each time it got longer and she started using proper nouns and you could understand what she wrote! Overall, this pen pal program was very fun and YES, you should continue it next year.
>
> *Pepper*

REFERENCES

Graves, D. *Investigating Nonfiction.* Portsmouth, New Hampshire: Heinemann, Educational Books, 1989.

Hansen, J. *When Writers Read.* Portsmouth, New Hampshire: Heinemann, Educational Books, 1989.

Smith, R. *Joining the Literacy Club.* Portsmouth, New Hampshire: Heinemann, Educational Books, 1989.

Wells, G. *The Meaning Makers: Children Learning Language and Using Language to Learn.* Portsmouth, New Hampshire: Heinemann, Educational Books, 1989.

Jean Fennacy, Deborah Manning, and Valerie Porter are classroom teachers in Fresno, California.

Linda Sheppard, Maryann Eeds,
and Mary Glover

Old Songs and Some Which Are New
One School's Revision

Sprawling at the foot of a hill on the northern edge of Kayenta, Arizona, is an old school, Kayenta Boarding School. As you stand in the rocky school yard, you can glimpse the nearest formations of Monument Valley to the northeast and the massive bulk of Black Mesa to the southeast. The classrooms and administrative offices are housed in three long cinder-block buildings, separated one from another by more of the rocky yard. About 350 children, kindergartners through eighth-graders, all boarders, inhabit the old-fashioned classrooms nine months of the year. The administration and teaching staff, half of whom are Navajo, are fluent in both English and Navajo. Some distance away from the offices and classrooms are the dorms and cafeteria, as well as maintenance buildings and housing for the staff. In this setting of powerful paradox, grandeur and wholeness juxtaposed with decline and isolation, the staff of Kayenta Boarding School sought a new way of educating their students while preserving and regaining their ancient heritage.

COMING TO KNOW STORY THROUGH READING AND WRITING

Having heard of successes of other Navajo schools using the whole language approach, the Kayenta staff was committed to trying methods that might be more successful with their own students. Many saw their current curriculum as fragmented and alienating to their Navajo students, whose culture valued the opposite—a holistic ethos and a sense of tribal history and community. The whole language teaching plan appealed to them.

For two intense weeks we talked, listened, read, wrote, and lived with the teachers and staff at Kayenta Boarding School. Three groups of primary, middle-grade, and junior-high teachers and aides worked together daily to develop a plan for implementing holistic education with their own students. Sessions with these adults, which included writing workshops, literature study, and scholarly pursuits that grew out of personal interests, ran as a whole language classroom might. We talked together in class and wrote to one another in dialogue journals after class. We set about to live together as a community of learners.

The first week's focus was on writing and telling stories. These began to emerge during writing workshop. Geneva wrote a piece about her work with the girls' basketball team. Lucy wrote about the special cake that was baked for the celebration accompanying her daughter's first menstrual period. Arlene wrote about when, as a five-year-old, she felt so desperate for something sweet to eat that she and her older sister not only ate an entire honeycomb of wild honey but, when that was gone, ate also the sweet white bee grubs.

Personal stories, powerful and empowering, came out of our literature study dialogues during the second week as well. In our discussion of the sea adventure *Call It Courage,* Katherine told two very different stories brought to her mind by her reading of the novel and the ensuing class dialogue. She told about when, as a teenager, she and a friend were ordered out of the water for inadvertently paddling among Navy warships during her first (and last!) visit to San Diego. Her other story was a wrenching description of the daily sense of loss she feels from the death of her husband, who died as a young man some twenty years ago. She likened her loss to that of the boy Mafatu, who into manhood mourns his mother, who died when he was only a few years old.

The power and universality of story was a big part of all that we experienced in Kayenta. In fact, our first major presentation to the staff that second week centered around the reasons people read (adapted from Page and Pinnell, 1979), and we introduced books of all kinds at that time. We focused on the possibilities for opening other worlds to the Kayenta students through experiences with books. In this presentation we discussed the importance of reading aloud from books written to inform. We stressed the pleasure and enjoyment we get from a book that can make us laugh, or cry, or experience a thrill of fear together—as well as the sense of community we get from sharing such experiences. Moments of pure identification also occurred as we talked of how books help, as Page and Pinnell say, to represent and make sense of life experiences. Paula Fox' s *Moonlight Man* (the story of a young girl who waits and waits for her father to pick her up from her boarding school before finding that alcohol has again caused him to forget her) caused several to share similar childhood experiences of being set down by the school bus in the vast high desert around Kayenta and waiting and wondering if anyone would ever come to get them. And when Robert Munsch' s *Love You Forever* was read, all the mothers cried, just as they do in any audience.

We had wondered if we should try to focus our talk about books on those written by or for Native Americans. But we found there were not many books written expressly for Navajo children, and even fewer written by writers who are knowledgeable about Navajo culture. Instead we all focused on the power of story in general, trusting that books written by word artists would strike universal responsive chords no matter how disparate our backgrounds and environments. Our hunches were confirmed. In fact, one of the major literary experiences of the group centered on the adventures and mishaps of Steig's heroic mouse Abel, who, marooned on an island, discovers previously untapped sources of inner strength.

We focused on three aspects of literature-based literacy programs: reading aloud every day to all the students at every grade level, providing time for the students to read extensively on their own every day, and organizing for more intensive study of literature in literature study groups. It was in a demonstration of one of these groups that we decided to use a book with an expressly Navajo theme and setting. The school had several copies of Miska Miles's *Annie and the Old One* (illustrated by Peter Parnall). This Newberry honor-winning book tells the story of a little girl whose grandmother tells her that when the rug now on the loom is finished, she will die. The tension of the book revolves around Annie's attempts to keep the rug from being finished. Most of the teachers who read this book for the literature study demonstration were Navajo, and most responded to the story as story, moved by the little girl's love for her grandmother and by her realization that she could not stop time. But Martha Garrison, daughter of a shaman and knowledgeable about the old ways herself, pointed out that the premise of the book was actually negated by Navajo culture. She said that no Navajo would discuss death at all—and certainly not with a child. It is something that is just not done. She also spoke of other inconsistencies and inaccuracies. For example, the coyote, called God's dog, represented as guarding the hogan, is actually considered a bad omen. And the illustrator includes plants, such as the ocotillo, not native to the high desert country of the reservation. Martha's extensive knowledge educated us all, including those who had grown up in Kayenta, but it also reinforced our feeling that there is no need (and, in fact, it is probably futile) to think that books chosen for special populations such as Navajo children growing up on an isolated reservation must reflect that environment and culture alone. Story is as old as humanity, and all humans respond to it. Literature can and does affirm one's culture and values, but it can also open up other worlds, other cultures, and other values for contemplation. The universality of literature connects us all.

Two entries from Geneva's journal illustrate the joy of growth and insight experienced during these two weeks of reading, writing, and living story. The first entry is from the day after she read her piece about the basketball team to our group:

> Linda, I learned something about myself yesterday. I can write. I didn't think I was a writer, but I am.
> *Geneva*

The second is from the next week, as we worked on making sense of the novels we were reading:

> Linda, I finished *Call It Courage* in just two days. Remember last week when I told you I was a writer? Well, I found out I can read too.
> *Geneva*

CHANGES AND FUTURE DIRECTIONS

When we returned to Kayenta a year later we wondered how things would be, knowing that it takes time and constant care for genuine transformation to take place. After a warm reception, we observed the beginnings of change. We noticed ideas set in motion to varying degrees, and we were met with a barrage of questions. From many individuals we felt a strong need for answers, and we often felt that the demands for solutions were well beyond our capabilities. Nevertheless, we went to work on the issues.

Our first step was to carry out a survey with the teaching staff and administration. Twenty-seven teachers and one administrator who responded had participated in the previous year's summer in-service. Five additional individuals had attended the October and November follow-ups. Their responses varied, but several patterns emerged. Since the whole language curriculum had been initiated the staff noticed the following:

•The children were more verbal:

"The students were more open and talkative....There was more freedom of asking and more respect for teachers and aides....The students are outspoken, especially the kindergartners. They cannot shut their mouths. They learn together. When I asked them a question, they all had their hands up for an answer."

•There was more real reading and writing going on:

"[The students had] better abilities to write about family, friends, travel, and soon...we had an abundance of writing taking place....The one change I noticed the most was in my reading group. We worked really well with the literature study with the more advanced reading groups. They were so into reading I couldn't keep up with them. Also our writing project. The students were more willing to write, and some were whipping up good writing. When given an option, they always wanted to write."

•For some staff members attitudes about teaching shifted:

"I have had a chance to become more involved with the students. I work with the students as a guide rather than being a director....I got to be more creative and flexible in my teaching this past year, so I had fun and enjoyed teaching even more....I felt closer to my students and vice-versa....Teaching seemed less organized but much more student oriented....Teaching was more fun."

•Many of the staff felt a greater sense of unity with others:

"Among the staff there appears to be much more cooperation and support....Teachers are talking to one another and sharing their experiences in what is happening to them when teaching whole language....We are now a closer-knit group and have a bond—whereas (most of us!) before, we did our own thing. We show more interest in others' work and accomplishments....Staff are more open and willing to share and discuss different things to promote a better environment for our school."

•There was a change in students' attitudes:

"The students were more relaxed and comfortable....The students are more in control of their learning....Students seem to care more about learning, had fewer discipline problems and were willing to share and work together....The students' attitudes towards listening, following directions, experimenting, understanding, and knowing became more sincere and realistic than just having to pass the grade or time. The students' self-confidence, self-worth, and their desire to learn and know changed....They were taking risks and not afraid of trying something new."

Aside from the apparent successes, changes in attitude, and encouraging growth, many problems still remained:

• More time was needed to continue practicing and learning about whole language methodology.

• More books, supplies, equipment, and materials were necessary in order to carry out daily classroom studies in the best way possible.

• Many of the staff felt the need for a stronger and clearer commitment of leadership from the administration.

• Further training and programs, specifically in whole language, would strengthen and enhance their work.

• More time and effort were needed to bring further unity to the staff, particularly across the different grade levels.

Although the difficulties were many and often appeared insurmountable, at the time we returned there still seemed to be an air of hope at Kayenta Boarding School. Many individuals were starting to make connections between the theory they had learned and their classroom practices. There was a sense of commitment on many of the teachers' parts and a willingness to continue. Most important, many believed that you can make a difference and good things are possible.

OLD SONGS AND SOME WHICH ARE NEW

In addition to the changes we observed with the Kayenta Boarding School faculty, another happy system of connections occurred for us as members of the in-service team as we lived the story of being there together. The experience stretched us as we worked to explain what we knew. It helped us distill our knowledge and renew our commitment to our work with our own students. The teachers at Kayenta Boarding School enabled us to see the worthwhileness of our ideas through their trust in what we taught them. The stories we told made sense to them and helped us to see that our stories had a universal appeal. This made us feel capable in a new way, knowing that we all shared a common goal. We could see ourselves more clearly in this remote and exotic place, away from our familiar surroundings.

One of the most valuable benefits of the experience was the opportunity for intensive extended dialogue with each other. As professionals and friends we were able to reflect and revise what we thought and knew. The time together, experiencing the magic of the Monument Valley area, enriched what we could bring to our Navajo colleagues.

As persons striving to do better in stewarding children, we all connected as members of families and communities that were both wildly different in some ways and exactly the same in many, many others. Our time with the Kayenta Boarding School faculty helped us to see what is possible when people work together to make sense out of living and learning. It was as if the new "songs" we brought allowed their old ones to come forth once again. By helping others to sing their song, we also began to hear our own. In the end, we had an exchange. An exchange of story, an exchange of song, and best of all, an exchange of gifts—the gift of a new way to see old truths.

REFERENCES

Fox, Paula. *Moonlight Man.* New York: Dell, 1988.

Miles, Miska. *Annie and Old One.* Boston: Little, Brown & Company, 1985.

Munsch, Robert. *Love You Forever.* Willowdale, Ontario: Firefly Books, 1982.

Sperry, Armstrong. *Call It Courage.* New York: MacMillan, 1990.

Steig, William. *Abel's Island.* New York: Farrar, Straus & Giroux, 1985.

Linda Sheppard teaches kindergarten at the Maryland School in Phoenix. Maryann Eeds is a professor at Arizona State University in Tempe. Mary Glover is a classroom teacher at the Awakening Seed School in Tempe.

Alexa Lindquist-Sandmann
and Joanne E. Herrmann

————————◆◆◆————————

Research Finds a Classroom
Firsthand Accounts From the Researcher and the Teacher

We took a journey into classroom research, Alexa wearing the researcher's hat and Joanne wearing the teacher's hat. Of course, other teachers and researchers would not take an identical journey, but our hope is that reading about our experience might encourage you to take your own journey into the realm of classroom-based research—research that looks at how real teachers nurture real students as they explore the purposes of real reading and real writing in real classrooms. Only these kinds of classrooms provide the research environment so necessary to learn how further to empower students and their teachers.

First, Alexa tells her story, the mechanics of finding Joanne and her classroom, in "Becoming a Researcher." Next, we tell our story, the issues we addressed initially, as well as those we discussed as the year progressed in "Resolving the Issues." Finally, Joanne tells of the unanticipated benefits of having had a researcher in her classroom in "Realizing the Benefits."

BECOMING A RESEARCHER: ALEXA'S STORY

In April of 1986, I began searching for a classroom in which to do my doctoral research the following fall because I wanted to begin my research on the first day of school. I was not sure where to begin. In Cincinnati in 1986, the writing process was not as well established as it is now, and I knew that finding a classroom that fit my requirements was not going to be easy.

I was looking for a classroom where the children were empowered to make choices about their writing. This meant that I was looking for a district where the teachers were empowered to make decisions about how their students would be permitted and encouraged to go about their learning; student empowerment follows teacher empowerment. Because I wanted to look at how students' choices affected their writing processes and products, I needed a writing community that followed the principles Donald Graves describes in *Writing: Teachers and Children at Work* (1983). I expected that the children would be able to choose their own topics and have ample and regular time for writing; would have many opportunities to have conferences, both with their peers and their teacher; would be assisted with revision; and would be provided with opportunities for "publishing."

These requirements were critical because I wanted to learn how fourth-grade students go about writing. I intended to watch four students, two of the stronger writers and two of the weaker writers, and their patterns of interaction with their peers and teacher. I wanted to know if ability affected writing patterns, and if it did, to discern how it did, ultimately considering the effects these patterns had on the writing itself.

With these requirements in mind, the chairman of my doctoral committee made several inquiries for me about finding a classroom in my own district, a district known for its academic excellence. Despite the obvious advantage I had in having someone inquire who already had established a working relationship with the district, the answer to the inquiries was negative. I was invited to review the writing files of the district's students, but since the schools recently had been inundated with researchers, my ongoing presence in a classroom would not be permitted. Frankly, I was quite disappointed. I was disappointed at not having available to me a valuable site, as well as one that would have been geographically close. Since I would be making two or three visits per week for an entire school year, proximity was a consideration.

On my own then, I decided to contact another district. I knew this one was committed to writing because many of its teachers had been participants in the Ohio Writing Project. I spoke with the principal of the elementary school and was surprised to find out that while the district was indeed committed to writing, the kind of writing process I had expected and needed to observe was not in practice at that school.

My third attempt proved fruitful. I chose a district that I thought valued writing and called the elementary principal. I remember vividly my sense of excitement when, after I explained what kind of classroom I needed, she said she thought she knew just the place. The principal recognized that to be part of a research project takes a particular kind of teacher. The principal knew Joanne was that kind of teacher, a judgment with which I have always agreed fully. Without naming Joanne, of course, the principal agreed to talk with her and ask her if she would be interested. Obviously she was. She called me the next day.

From the first, I felt comfortable with Joanne. We spoke on the telephone and made arrangements to meet two days later. Arriving a few minutes early, I waited in the hall until she could talk with me. At the same time I was trying to be unobtrusive, she stopped readying her students for their walk to art class, asked me if I was Alexa, and then introduced me to her class. She explained to her students that I would be doing research in her class next year and then, after cajoling the slowpokes into getting in line, walked the class to art, chatting with the students about various projects as they went.

Her enthusiasm in introducing me to her students seemed a good indication that she was truly interested in my study; genuine interest would mean that the research would go as smoothly as possible. As they walked into the hallway, I watched Joanne's warm and caring responses to her students as well as their responses to her. While I had not had the opportunity to see Joanne work with students during writing workshop, her basic nature, even in that brief glimpse of teacher-student relationships as I stood outside the door, gave me some concrete experiences as to her perspective of students. My intuition told me that I had found just the kind of teacher I needed for my study.

A formal part of my entry to Joanne's classroom was the signing of contracts. One contract needed to be signed by the principal and the teacher. In the form of a letter (*Figure 1*), I introduced myself, described the purpose of my research, and then specified how I would go about gathering data. In the next two paragraphs I specified the safety issues for the school and the teacher: (1) I would protect the identity of all participants in any writing I did; (2) the principal, teacher, or parents had the right to terminate the study at any time; and (3) if on any day I came it was inconvenient for me to stay, I would need only to be told and I would return another day. Finally, I made an offer to present the results of the research project to the principal and teacher, if they so desired. The principal's and teacher's signatures were obtained on the written contract (*Figure 2*) before I started observing.

Additionally, I needed to have parents' permission for me to observe, take field notes about, and videotape their children. Again, a letter (*Figure 3*) introduced me, described the purpose of my research, specified their children's role in that research, and provided the same safety assurances that had been given to the principal and teacher. The written consent form (*Figure 4*) provided for two levels of participation in the study; a student could be a study participant and be videotaped, with the understanding that the videotapes would be shown only to limited audiences of scholars for study purposes, or a student could be a participant in the study with the understanding that any videotapes with that student in them would not be shown to anyone. A third option, of course, was that the student not be allowed to participate.

Contract in hand and consent forms distributed to the students on the first day of school in August, I began my research. Until our author party the first Monday in June, I was a part of Joanne's language arts class on writing days, two or three times a week. I would try to get to school just when the language arts class was entering Joanne's room, but if I arrived a few minutes earlier and walked quietly to my desk in the back of the room, Joanne's science students just said hi and then quickly went back to work. I would set up the video camera and get out my paper and pen.

The students would come in, snack in hand, some saying hi, others searching for me to share a story, and still others obviously unconcerned whether I was there or not. Joanne would begin class, usually reading aloud. Joanne's minilesson would come next, and then we would all write, sustained silent writing (SSW) for at least twenty minutes. I wrote, too, but I must confess most times I was writing field notes.

Afterwards, students would share their work with a partner, a small group, or the whole group, depending on Joanne's and the students' negotiated agenda. All this time, the video camera was on, and some days, individual students wore a remote microphone that was connected with the camera so that I could record conversations that occurred anywhere in the room.

If I thought something was happening during SSW that I needed to see more closely than my seating would allow, I got up to look; otherwise,

I stayed seated during SSW and wrote, limiting my roaming to sharing time. I rarely walked with pen and paper in hand because this particular class was so animated that I did not want to add fuel to their dramatic fires. Instead, I wandered throughout the room, asked questions, and then made a beeline back to my desk where I recorded the information.

The students accepted me readily. On my sixth visit, two students asked to have a conference with me. When I introduced the video camera a few visits later, both Joanne and I thought it attracted little attention. I wondered if the students were already so used to me that the camera seemed a small intrusion. Since I had been a part of their writing workshop from the first day and because I continued to observe them only on writing workshop days, I hypothesized that I had become part of their schema for writing. When I tested this hypothesis with Joanne, she concurred.:

RESOLVING THE ISSUES: OUR STORY

Wrangling with the mechanics of becoming and being a researcher, as well as inviting and living with a researcher for nine months, was made easier for each of us because certain ground rules were established before observations were begun. Anyone considering a research collaboration should establish ground rules, for they created a firm foundation for us and contributed to the easy rapport we developed. These discussions did not eliminate hurdles; rather, we could more easily overcome any roadblocks because we had established an ongoing dialogue.

One absolute superseded all of the issues that follow. For both of us, the students' welfare was paramount. Beyond this essential understanding, we had a solid foundation to begin resolving other issues for two more reasons: First, Alexa was not changing the natural order of events in Joanne's classroom, but would be observing the writing process to which Joanne was already professionally and personally committed; second, based on what we both knew about the writing process, we believed that research could help us discover some new truths about the writing process and fourth-graders.

Thinking we both clearly understood our roles, we were ready to begin. Even though Joanne intellectually understood that Alexa would be in her classroom to observe the students, she could not overcome the feeling that Alexa was really there to evaluate her abilities as a teacher. Joanne felt particularly uncomfortable since she was working out the details of a relatively new format, the writing workshop. This discomfort was intensified by the presence of a video camera that recorded her every word! Part of this intimidation dealt with Joanne's own preconceived notion of what a researcher was; Alexa did not threaten Joanne, but her credentials did.

Wanting to make everything about her classroom conducive to the "best research ever," Joanne bent over backwards to accommodate Alexa. Ironically, she made Alexa's job more difficult because Joanne's deference to her perception of Alexa's wishes altered the natural order of events, which Alexa wanted to see. To illustrate: Joanne would have created her lesson for the day. Rather than carrying on with business as usual, Joanne would ask Alexa for her input: "Will this best help you to see what you need to observe today?" Alexa would then be tempted to voice an opinion, yet in doing so, she, too, would alter the natural sequence of events. Joanne is sure this behavior eventually would have driven us both crazy if she had not reached a turning point in mid-October.

This pivotal point in our working relationship occurred one day after Joanne had presented her lesson and some of the children had experienced difficulty in grasping the concept. This did not surprise Joanne because it was a concept that usually took several lessons for the students to grasp. What flabbergasted Joanne was Alexa's genuine surprise: "I can't believe the class had so much trouble with the lesson today. I thought any fourth-grader could handle that."

At this point, Joanne reclaimed her classroom. She explicitly acknowledged that she had her areas of expertise and Alexa had hers. Joanne was the teacher with the knowledge of fourth-graders and their needs; she no longer would privilege Alexa's university position. This new perspective made our jobs much easier.

For Alexa, from the beginning, the critical issue was the difficulty she found in keeping her researcher hat on. Alexa found it much more inviting and comfortable to slip her teacher hat on, particularly because, for these students, as it would be with any, an adult in a classroom who is not a parent or the principal is considered a teacher. These students had no previous experience with a researcher and so had no concept of how that person might be unlike a teacher; they treated Alexa like a teacher, which Joanne encouraged and Alexa did not discourage—up to a point. Actually, Alexa enjoyed the role, having always loved being a classroom teacher. In fact, it made the entry into this classroom easier for her because it meant she, too, had a role for which everyone—students, other teachers, and even the administration—had a definition.

In late October, some resolution of this teacher/researcher dilemma evolved after a discussion with a university colleague. Alexa realized that she had to take more of a researcher stance if she were to collect the kinds of information she needed to address her research question. While Alexa's having conferences with students early in the year could be explained as aid in getting the writing workshop going, her continuing to do so would change the natural order of writing in Joanne's classroom, something which would compromise the research.

Another important issue for Alexa was use of class time. Since Joanne had five morning and three afternoon language-arts periods each week, Alexa could not possibly be present during all of them. Knowing Alexa's need to see students as they were writing and her ability to observe in the mornings, Joanne relegated spelling and district-required editing of prescribed sentences to the afternoon, when Alexa would not be present. Since language-arts periods in the morning were an hour and fifteen minutes, Joanne began the year by dividing the time between reading and writing. By late November, though, Joanne decided to focus her attention on reading on days Alexa was not there and on writing on the days she was; thus, the time Alexa spent at school was maximized.

Another issue involved balancing the amount of time Alexa spent with the focal four students versus the other students in the class. Since Alexa had never announced that she was researching the writing patterns of only four students, and since the purpose of this research was studying these four writers within a writing community, she had to make it appear that no one student was favored over another. Even though Alexa did talk with them, had the video camera focused on them, and asked the focal four students to wear the remote microphone proportionally more than the other students in the class, we are as certain as possible that the students were unaware of it since Alexa interacted with everyone. Sam did feel that Alexa was a little slow in choosing him to wear the remote microphone, though, and Alexa arranged for him to wear the microphone during her next visit.

Still another issue for Alexa, professionally as well as personally, was a conscious effort not just to take what she needed from Joanne, her class, and the school. Alexa tried to give something in return. One way was to be Joanne's substitute on several occasions. Another was to take care of the monthly book-club orders, and on one occasion she hung paper-stuffed whales from the ceiling panels. Perhaps surprising, though, is the fact that the most important benefits of Alexa's presence were the ones which were not explicitly given or anticipated.

JOANNE'S STORY: REALIZING THE BENEFITS

Originally, the additional classroom noise, an inherent characteristic of student interaction during the writing process, was an issue for me. Even teachers who believe that "constructive" noise is possible and, indeed, that student interaction is important to cognitive growth are still aware of how other teachers and administrators might perceive it. Consequently, my comfort level was challenged much of the year, despite the fact that I knew conferences were critical to the writing process. My comfort level would have been challenged whether Alexa had been there or not, although I did broaden my level of acceptability because she was. For example, despite the rule about not talking during SSW, I did allow quiet conversations if they did not disturb other students.

Alexa told me she was particularly thankful for this initial bending of the rule since it allowed her to observe naturally spontaneous interactions during the process of writing. As the year progressed, however, it became increasingly clear to both of us how important these interactions were. Tommy, one of the four focal students, and his writing partner, David, seemed unable to sustain their writing without talking during SSW. The decision to allow them to talk quietly while writing was what enabled them to produce most effectively in writer's workshop.

Another day, Alexa reported that her researcher's heart stopped when I told her that I had asked Allison, another of the focal four, and her writing partner, Beth, to sit apart for a few weeks. I knew that if the girls were forced to sit apart, Alexa could not see their natural interaction as they wrote, but I had no alternative. This decision was easier for Alexa to accept because she understood what had precipitated it and as a teacher happened to agree with my decision, but even if she had not, my decision would have remained. As a researcher, though, I know she breathed much more easily when Allison and Beth needed only a few days to settle down and so were granted permission to sit together once again.

Amazingly, my concern about noise became a benefit. I no longer worry about people's perceptions in witnessing the constructive buzz that so often exists in my classroom. Armed with analysis of Alexa's data, I can readily explain that students were on task at least 89 percent of the time. In writing this manuscript, I realized how many more opportunities I give my students because of my continuing comfort with a higher-than-normal noise level. Each year since our research year I have allowed my students to take greater responsibility for one another's learning as well as for their own. I no longer view this productive hubbub as a threat to my classroom control but more as a logical and desirable result of process learning.

Another unexpected benefit of having a researcher in my classroom was the comfort the children developed with sharing their work. True, some of their comfort occurred because we were a community, but I truly believe that much of it can be attributed to the presence of a researcher. The children felt honored to have a researcher in their classroom, and the prestige they felt was reflected in their willingness to share in both large and small groups. They were eager to share in order to seek improvement for their writing, as well as to celebrate a successful publication. This group loved the attention of another adult, and Alexa's presence seemed to motivate them to work harder. David expressed the feelings of several: "This is my chance to be famous!" He would then grin broadly and resume writing feverishly.

Alexa's presence as a researcher contributed to my own growth as well. I did a 180-degree turn in my own perception of research. By January I found myself regularly jotting notes in my log about the children. This note taking and record keeping was a significant area of growth for me. Previously, I had considered note taking to be Alexa's domain. Imagine my surprise at my newfound compulsion to start keeping anecdotal records. Imagine Alexa's surprise when I practically thrust myself upon her with my hunches, wonderings, and suppositions about the children. She must have been doubly surprised when I began to talk in terms of *our* research. Research had become demystified for me. I, who once had dodged the penetrating eye of the video camera, now wanted this research year to continue forever.

Of course our year together had to end, but its benefits empowered me in many ways. I felt validated. My work had more meaning. I gained experience, but more than that, I learned to value my own inner resources and capabilities. I also rediscovered the value of asking questions.

This new outlook of a classroom teacher/researcher prompted me to seek more course work in whole language when I learned of a master's in writing program featuring Nancie Atwell and Mary Ellen Giacobbe.

Another benefit that neither of us could have anticipated was the fervent desire I developed to encourage others to attempt whole language classrooms. With another colleague, I formed a writing support group for my school district. Then, I became involved in teaching writing workshops to teachers in a three-district area. Several teachers now use a writing process approach, and many others have adopted at least some of our practices, which reflect process teaching and a whole language approach to learning.

Three years later, I am still reaping the benefits. I now have children in my classes who are experienced in writing and who have been immersed in literature since kindergarten and grade 1. When Alexa began her research, my fourth-graders had no idea what we meant by writing workshop. As a matter of fact, my notes in our first few weeks revealed that about 25 percent of the fourth-graders were drawing and finding ways to avoid writing; I do not have one reluctant writer in my current third-grade class.

I am in the fortunate position of being able to follow the development of my former students as well. I see the fourth- and fifth-grade teachers regularly and hear of my students' accomplishments. I enjoy seeing the published writings on display throughout the building. As my colleagues share anecdotes, successes, and questions, I often reflect how our perception of process writing might differ if our district had not allowed one researcher to visit just one classroom.

ALexa Lindquist-Sandmann is a faculty member in education at Northern Kentucky University. Joanne E. Herrmann is a third-grade teacher at Indian Hill Elementary School in Cincinnatti.

August 26, 1986

_____, Principal
_____ Elementary School
___ _____ Road
Cincinnati, Ohio 45___

Dear _____:

As you know when I spoke with you this spring, I am a doctoral student in Curriculum and Instruction at the University of Cincinnati and am about to begin the research for my dissertation. Because of your help, Mrs. _____ has agreed to allow me to conduct my research in her class. We've had a chance to talk and I couldn't be more pleased. Her interest and enthusiasm are wonderful.

Since I spoke with you, the plan for my research has become more specific as it is finalized, and so I would like to explain the details to you. Because of my interest in how children learn to write, I plan to observe the patterns of interaction of fourth graders of different writing abilities (as determined by Mrs. _____ and myself) with their peers and their teacher during composing sessions within their classroom.

Throughout the 1986-87 school year, I plan to be in Mrs. _____'s fourth-grade classroom on specified, mutually convenient times, probably three times a week for about two hours. I will focus my attention on four students, but will note any interactions these four have with other students in the class. In addition to my observations, I plan occasionally to interview the children and the teacher to check my impressions and findings—at their convenience, of course. Sometimes, I will use a tape recorder during these interviews. I also will be making copies of their writing and making videotapes of the students' interactions.

I will protect the identity of all participants, that is, you, the teacher, the children, and the school, in anything I write for publication.

You, the teacher, the children, and their parents have the right to terminate the study at any time. In addition, if on any day I come to observe, it turns out to be inconvenient for anyone, please tell me and I will return another day. I will present the results of the project to you and the teacher in the form of a written report, if you so desire.

Thank you for your attention and consideration in this matter. I'm looking forward to beginning this project.

Sincerely,

Alexa L. Sandmann

FIGURE 1

WRITTEN CONTRACT

We, the undersigned, have read and understand the accompanying explanations of Alexa L. Sandmann's research project at _____ Elementary School and mutually agree with the content and conduct of this project.

Date:_____

_____
(Principal)

Date:_____

_____
(Teacher)

FIGURE 2

August 26, 1986

Dear Parents:

As a doctoral student in Curriculum and Instruction at the University of Cincinnati, I am ready to do the research for my dissertation. As a program requirement, and under the supervision of Dr. Chet Laine and my doctoral committee, I am to design and perform a study of my own. Because of my interest in how children learn to write and how their development affects their writing, I would like to observe the patterns of interaction of eight fourth-graders with their peers and their teacher during composing sessions in their classroom.

I asked Mrs. _____ to choose eight children of varying writing abilities, and since your child was one of the eight, I need your permission before I may begin my observations. In addition, I would occasionally like to interview your child to check out my impressions and findings, at the teacher's and your child's convenience, of course. Sometimes I will use a tape recorder during these interviews. I will also make copies of your child's writing. Further, I will be making videotapes of the students' interactions.

I will protect the identity of your child in any research papers I write by giving him or her a different name. At the end of the study, I will make available to you a copy of the final report that I write, if you would like one.

If you permit your child to be a part of my study, you have the right to terminate his or her participation at any time. All you would need to do is notify me or Mrs. _____.

I hope you will allow me to observe your child as a part of this study. In either case, I would greatly appreciate it if you would check the appropriate line on the accompanying sheet and return it to Mrs. _____ by the end of the week. If you have any questions, please call me at either 475-3561 or 489-1577.

Thank you for your consideration.

Sincerely,

Alexa L. Sandmann

FIGURE 3

WRITTEN CONSENT FORM

I, the undersigned, have read and understand the accompanying explanations of Alexa L. Sandmann's research project at _____ Elementary School.

_____ I give my child permission to participate and be videotaped, with the videotapes shown only to limited audiences of scholars for study purposes.

_____ I give my child permission to participate and be videotaped, but I request that the tapes with my child on them not be shown to limited audiences of scholars for study purposes.

_____ I do not give my child permission to participate.

_____
(Child's name)

_____
(Signature of parent or guardian)

_____
(Date)

FIGURE 4

BEVERLY J. BRUNEAU

Two Kindergarten Teachers Developing Whole Language Programs

STORIES OF TEACHER GROWTH AND CURRICULAR CHANGE

In an important article surveying recent research on young children's development of reading, William Teale wrote that he believed many early childhood teachers would welcome the new reading research that proposes that children learn literacy in an active, playful fashion, an approach towards teaching long embraced by teachers of young children (1987). Such teachers, Teale suggested, would be pleased to move away from a textbook and worksheet approach typically used in kindergarten classrooms. This paper presents two case stories of teachers attempting to move toward whole language instruction. One teacher, Sandra, was very successful in implementing a whole language program. The other teacher, Marlene, was able to make some small but definitive steps toward engaging her children in more meaningful print experiences. Each teacher's story illustrates not only important curricular changes but also the process of teacher development as both teachers developed their ability to empower their decision making as teachers of young children.

WHY TEACHER CHANGE MAY BE DIFFICULT

To change one's teaching from following a skills-based program to building a whole language program which focuses on children's own learning is an enormous change. An important difference between a skills-based classroom and a whole language classroom is the role of the teacher. A skills-based program requires the teacher to follow a prescribed curriculum. A teacher in a whole language classroom takes a more active role in planning learning experiences based on individual children's understanding of written language (Bruneau, 1988). To feel confident to begin planning one's own curriculum after following a prescribed reading program can be an extremely difficult task for many teachers (Shannon, 1987).

For many teachers, the move to establishing a whole language program may be a move they wish to make. However, they may have great difficulty in doing so because whole language is based on a different understanding of the process of learning literacy than that held by readiness programs. Do teachers perceive children's learning as occurring through active hypothesis building through immersion in meaningful text, or do teachers view literacy learning as occurring through mastery of a predetermined sequence of skills? A useful starting place in developing whole language curriculum for teacher educators and teachers themselves is to understand the perspective teachers hold about teaching reading and writing (Bruneau, 1988; Bruneau and Ambrose, 1989). To better understand the perspectives of teachers requires an understanding of beliefs, knowledge of teaching, and the context or setting in which each individual teacher works.

TEACHER BELIEFS

Traditional teacher-education programs rarely are concerned with thoughts or current practice of teachers (Falk, 1987). However, if teacher learning is perceived as active, constructive learning, the kind of learning that empowers teacher development, teachers' thoughts and beliefs become important (Feiman-Nemser and Floden, 1986; Harste, Woodward and Burke, 1984). This seems particularly pertinent when helping teachers move from a skills-based to whole language instruction. For example, Taylor, Blum, and Logsdon (1985) found that only one-half of the kindergarten teachers with whom they worked were able to implement whole language practice into their classrooms. They suggest that difference in beliefs among the classroom teachers and whole language approach toward teaching may explain why some could not change.

Further, Shannon's (1983) research has indicated that many teachers believe that basal readers provide a systematic approach toward reading instruction that is superior to individual teacher-planned instruction. A teacher who believes that basals offer a better planned program than one he or she could develop would have difficulty relinquishing the basal reader. Clearly, an understanding of individual teacher beliefs, especially about how reading develops and how best to teach it, becomes an important consideration for teacher educators attempting to assist teachers in developing a whole language program.

RESTRUCTURING KNOWLEDGE OF TEACHING

Along with their individual beliefs, teachers have also constructed knowledge of how to teach in their classrooms. An experienced teacher may have developed firmly established routines based on his or her understanding of how to teach reading and writing. Routines based on a skills-based approach would have to be discarded and replaced by new procedures based on a revised understanding of the process of how young children learn literacy to read. Giving up comfortable ways of teaching can be frustrating for many experienced teachers (Duffy and Roehler, 1989).

Duffy and Roehler (1989) have suggested that the revision of teaching routines or procedures based on a restructured understanding of teaching reading needs to occur along four dimensions. First, teachers need information to help understand why a change in teaching reading is important and to further understand how the process of learning to read has been reconceptualized from a skills-based to a language-based process. Second, procedural information is needed to allow teachers to "put into action" new teaching procedures or strategies. Teachers need to know the "how" of how to do it. Third, teachers need to develop the ability to think about their planning of lessons, to put together all the factors that allow for children to learn in new ways. And fourth, teachers need to develop ability to mediate planned lessons, to adapt "in action" to responses from children. Duffy and Roehler (1989) emphasize that the process of building new teaching knowledge is a complex, time-consuming endeavor.

TEACHER CONTEXTS

Not only must teachers' beliefs and knowledge be taken into consideration when attempting to help teachers develop a new kind of program, but the context in which teachers work must also be considered as an aspect that either helps or inhibits teacher empowerment. Joyce, Hersh, and McKibbin (1983) state that teachers experience constraints imposed from both outside and inside their school. Outside constraints such as state and local government curricular regulations and teacher accountability formats as well as expectations of particular groups of parents affect teachers' ability to implement new change. Within schools, directives from the building principal as well as indirect pressure from other teachers may limit the freedom teachers believe they have to be innovative within their own classrooms.

For teachers to make a curricular change, particularly a change reflecting a major conceptual reorganization of how children learn, is a difficult task. Attention to individual teacher beliefs, knowledge of teaching, and the particular context of the school are important aspects of a teacher-development program. Just as a whole language literacy program requires teachers to base learning experiences on the prior understanding of print of individual children, it also seems teacher educators need to focus on the understandings and realities of the individual teachers with whom they work if they are to assist teachers in controlling their own development and their own teachers (Wildman & Niles, 1987).

INDIVIDUAL TEACHER STORIES

Based on the assumption that the process of developing a whole language program would be different for each teacher, two case studies of an implementation of a whole language program were conducted. Research questions which framed these investigations included

1. What kinds of curricular change based on whole language principles were the teachers able to implement?

2. What beliefs did the teachers appear to hold about teaching reading and writing to young children? Did these beliefs appear to facilitate or inhibit the change process?

3. What kinds of problems and concerns did the teachers have as they

engaged in the change process? What kinds of knowledge and support appeared helpful to the teachers as they attempted to solve these problems?

4. What particular constraints appeared to inhibit each teacher's development of a whole language program?

DATA COLLECTION AND ANALYSIS

Data were collected for these two case studies through participant observation and interviews and through written documents. The teacher educator played a more "active" participant role as she worked with Marlene modeling various teaching strategies in classroom. Although some modeling of teaching was done in working with Sandra, the teacher educator served mainly as a consultant, listening to Sandra's concerns and providing support through planning conferences. The participant role the teacher educator played with both teachers was what each teacher had requested. Open-ended interview questions were used during the interviews to elicit the participants' perceptions (Spradley, 1979). Written documents included work done by the children during the data collection period.

Data were analyzed through two methods, categorical analysis (Spradley, 1979) and discrepant case analysis (Erickson, 1986). The findings will be reported as two case studies of each of the individual teachers. They will focus on the beliefs, implementations, and problems and concerns facing each of the kindergarten teachers.

SANDRA

Sandra, at age 25, began her first year of teaching kindergarten at a university-based child-development center. She had previously taught first grade in a parochial school for two years and during this time taught reading and writing through following basal programs, as she was directed to do. As she began to plan for her kindergarten year, Sandra asked if she could replace the center's "letter of the week" program and "teach" literacy through a whole language approach as she had been taught in her undergraduate education program. The director of the center highly supported Sandra's curricular changes in literacy. Sandra asked for support and a teacher educator agreed to work together with her in helping her develop her own program.

Beliefs

Sandra held the following beliefs about teaching young children and teaching reading and writing to kindergarten children:

1. Students should be involved in active learning "using all of their senses to manipulate objects and come up with their own conclusions."

2. Teaching involves setting up the environment so that children can have choices among activities that interest them. The activities should be open-ended so that children may participate in a variety of "creative ways."

3. Children should be empowered to engage in learning activities of their own choosing. "Children learn most effectively when they have ownership over what they do."

4. The process of problem solving is most important. "I've been criticized for taking so long, but children learn best when they are able to solve their problems together."

5. "Reading is a meaning, not a decoding, activity."

6. Kindergarten children are not "ready for isolated phonics. They are not ready for skills. The process of learning to read begins with recognizing words in context."

7. Writing is important. "The way children learn is to use their own language and write it down."

8. "I can facilitate literacy learning through modeling reading and building confidence in children to take risks."

Sandra organized her classroom in a manner congruent with her expressed beliefs in allowing children choice and variety. For two hours each morning, children were given the opportunity to engage in a variety of centers of their own choosing—blocks, housekeeping, science, math, art, and a well-stocked library corner. Sandra also conducted two extended group periods, one in the morning and one in the afternoon, in which she read stories and led discussions on science and social studies topics. She would often engage children in problem solving during these periods. Discussions ranged from how best to share playground materials to extensive planning for a Thanksgiving dinner.

Implementations: Getting Started

Sandra began the year by creating a "print-rich environment." Centers and activities were labeled. Reading and writing materials were available at several centers. Children wrote grocery lists and bills in the housekeeping center, labeled their block constructions, and read labels placed on objects as they worked in the science center.

Sandra shared books enthusiastically with her children, showing them title pages and talking about authors and illustrators. Parents stated children would request books by favorite authors when visiting the library. Children often brought in books from home for Sandra to read. Sandra believed keeping the library corner filled with a variety of "good" children's books was important. During this period, children made class books about field trips they had taken. Each child drew a picture and dictated a sentence for a page in the book. Sandra also constructed a book of the children's favorite songs and finger plays. Children would often take this book and "read" the songs and poems to each other.

An author's corner was stocked with paper, pencils, crayons, and markers. Many children would choose to visit this center to make their own book. Children would often dictate messages to Sandra. Some children would write lists of words they knew how to spell, and others would, at times, copy words posted throughout the classroom.

Sandra began to integrate children's learning in science with reading and writing experiences. For example, one morning she introduced the children to a chart entitled "Will it dissolve?" Sandra listed a number of objects such as salt, sugar, raisins, rocks, and Cheerios. She then engaged the children in predicting whether they thought each object would dissolve in water and recorded the number of children predicting yes or no for each object. During the course of the week, children individually conducted this experiment and recorded their findings on a prepared chart.

Sandra was especially proud of these kinds of experiences. "This is the kind of activity I do best," she stated. Sandra excitedly reported that children were "reading" the charts. "I know that most of them wouldn't be able to read the words out of context, but they go up to that chart and say the words to each other." During the fall months, the classroom walls were filled with various charts and lists the children made through scientific observations.

Problems and Concerns

Generally, Sandra believed she was off to a good start. The children were enthusiastically involved in center work. She had weathered parent orientation, where she explained her whole language program as well as her daily curriculum. The overall parent response was enthusiastic and Sandra was pleased. However, as November began, Sandra was worried that she hadn't seen any invented spelling among the children's writing. "Invented spelling is supposed to develop from the children's drawings, isn't it?" she asked.

Although the children enthusiastically continued to draw and seek dictation for their pictures, they were very reluctant to try to write words. They wanted to know how to "write it correctly." Often they would ask each other for help and several children were able to supply information on spelling words "right." Sandra felt frustrated and asked for help.

At this point, the teacher educator modeled a few lessons to illustrate the process of invented spelling. "If you want to write all by yourself, you can listen for the sounds you hear and write the letters that say those sounds on paper." As a group, the children participated in "writing" simple stories such as, "I tk mi dog to the vet. Se gt a jot." (I took my dog to the vet. She got a shot.) Sandra began to ask children for sounds as she, too, modeled invented spelling while writing daily charts. Within the group situation, the children responded. However, in their own writing the children wanted the words "spelled right."

Sandra decided to try a group writing time. As she was currently teaching a science unit on the senses, she decided to have each child author a sense book, writing one sentence for each sense studied. Although the children engaged in invented spelling writing messages such as "I l k to se brs" (I like to see birds), Sandra was frustrated. "I feel like I am spoonfeeding. I say we are going to write. I encourage them to write, but many of them don't want to try." She also was not pleased with the whole group activity. "Some of them are just not really ready for this. What do I do with them?" Sandra decided not to continue with group writing time. It conflicted with her belief in allowing children to choose their own activity.

One late November morning, Sandra and the group were constructing an experience chart called "Things We Need to Do to Prepare for Our Feast." Obtaining ideas from the children, she listed necessary jobs for the children to share. As she wrote words, she also talked about sounds. "Mash potatoes. How do I know what letter to write for potato?" And the children as a group would respond correctly. As the lesson came to closure, one boy suggested they write a chart called "Manners for Our Feast." Sandra wrote the title on chart paper and asked the child if he would like to write his rule. She handed him the marker and he wrote, "DT TK W YR MS OPN" (Don't talk with your mouth open). Three more children eagerly volunteered their manner rules, writing their own messages. Invented spelling was accepted by the children.

Implementations: Taking Off

During the month of December, many children began to experiment with writing. Sandra believed that holiday letter writing in which children wrote notes and cards to each other served as a motivating force involving more and more children in writing "on their own." When children returned to school in January, each received a bound notebook to serve as a journal. Sandra told the children they needed to write in it at least once each week. Sandra believed this allowed children to have freedom of choice yet still spend some time in journal writing. Sandra often spent time in the writing center, assisting children in listening for sounds and writing their words. She stated she thought these individual learning times were valuable but also added it was hard to spend this amount of quality time with all twenty-five children.

Sandra began to include more predictable books in the library corner so that children could gain a sense of "reading" the stories. During center time, children often read to each other. Children volunteered to read stories at group time. In March, Sandra reported excitedly that Martin, a child who previously had shown little interest in books, stated he wanted to read a predictable book to the class. "He read the book to me and then read it over and over during center time. At group time, he read the story and the children clapped and cheered."

During this period with so many children engaged in reading and writing, Sandra worried about the few children, such as Martin, who were reluctant to do so. "Those few who are not making good progress—what will happen to them in first grade?" Sandra knew that most children would move to first-grade programs where they would be grouped according to their ability to recognize letter names and sounds and read the sight words presented in the district's kindergarten program. Her concerns were further amplified by concerns of the parents who worried their children would be placed in "low groups" because they would not have the same kind of "phonic knowledge" as children who had gone to the district kindergarten (Bruneau, Rasinski, and Ambrose, 1989). The progress of these children posed a dilemma for Sandra. She did not want to teach children directly but feared if she did not her children would be "disadvantaged because they didn't know their letters." Sandra still wanted children to have ownership of their experiences but also wanted to see them more involved in print.

Because of her concerns about first grade, Sandra focused on knowledge of alphabet letters and their sounds as an indicator of growth among children. This sometimes caused her difficulty in identifying progress. For example, one girl, Bea, was unable to take a risk to write words she did not know how to spell. Through February, her writing consisted of writing her name, names of her family members, and words she could copy. During February, she began to write letter strings, followed in March by her first written story, "KKacpq ILAZG Vanz DIKK DYYD GHyA" (King gave flowers to the queen). Sandra, who was focusing on letter-sound correspondence, initially didn't see the tremendous breakthrough this was for Bea. Because she was so focused on worrying whether Bea would be able to identify letters in first grade, she needed reassurance that this was indeed a major step to be celebrated.

Because of her concern about progress, conferences between Sandra and the teacher educator focused on the products of students whom Sandra identified as "having problems." Sandra seemed to need reassurance that these children were indeed developing enthusiasm for reading. After he read his first storybook to the class, Sandra was encouraged to provide more opportunities for Martin to read and did not push him in writing at this time, a task that he hated. Interestingly, within the next month, Martin's drawings became more complex and his writing changed from "IWTWRMCO" (I want to work on my computer) to "JAt EDT MT YT CYeTY" (Giants eat meat when they're hungry). Sandra was delighted with this product, focusing on the sound-symbol association he had developed.

Summary

During the course of her first year, Sandra was able to engage her children enthusiastically in print through a whole language program. She had developed a conceptual basis for whole language through her under-graduate program. Her beliefs about teaching also supported a whole language approach to literacy learning, particularly beliefs about children reading through context and writing through seeing their own language written down.

Not only were Sandra's beliefs about reading and writing congruent with a whole language approach, but her beliefs about children learning in general through active, self-generated, problem-solving learning provide support for a whole language curriculum. She also defined teaching as "facilitating learning" and believed that when she was interacting with children as they worked at different activities, she was indeed teaching. For Sandra, the one-on-one type of instruction she used in the writing center was a "valuable use of teacher time."

Sandra also began with the procedural knowledge of how to begin to implement the kind of teaching she wished to do. She knew how to set up and organize centers, knew how to introduce books to children, and knew how to use print continuously through the day to engage children in reading and writing activities. Sandra did have the overall knowledge to manage the flow of activities within her classroom that allowed children to engage individually in meaningful written-language experiences.

Sandra began the year with general knowledge of invented spelling. She fully expected her children to develop this ability. When she did not see it occurring, she asked for help in how to begin to facilitate this development. This was the only instance in which Sandra asked for someone to model a procedure for her. From limited modeling, Sandra quickly took over, beginning to emphasize listening for sounds as she continued to write lists and stories. In reflecting on the year, she said that in her second year she would feel more confident knowing that "it [invented spelling] would indeed happen."

Once Sandra believed most of her children were "well on their way," she asked for help with the few children who were not making "good progress." Here, she needed information on developmental stages in both reading and writing. This information provided her with confidence that the children were really progressing and would also serve as a springboard of the kinds of interactions she might continue to have with each child. Help in mediating work for children's assignments was a valued source of information for her at this time.

Sandra believed this year had been an "empowering" experience for her teaching. Sandra stated, "This has been the first year that I've felt I could teach in a way I felt was right for the children." Despite the fact that she felt empowered to teach whole language, she also was affected by very real constraints. Even though fully supported by her administrator, Sandra felt the pressure of the surrounding school district's requirements to prepare children who would be "ready" for first grade. Having taught first grade herself, Sandra knew exactly what those requirements were and worried that a few of her children would not "fit" into a first-grade program. Her own worry was compounded by concerns of parents who wished their students to be placed well as they started elementary school. This concern caused her to focus more on letter-sound relationships, and she was tempted to push some children into doing more writing. Even in a very supportive environment, expectations from outside the school were a tremendous source of anxiety during this teacher's first year of whole language instruction.

MARLENE

Marlene had been teaching for thirty-two years, twenty-nine years as a first-grade teacher. She had taught kindergarten during the last three years, having been requested to do so by her principal. Marlene's principal believed she would be able to provide a "less paper-and-pencil kindergarten program," which he stated he believed was important for young children. Marlene was one of four kindergarten teachers teaching in a small-town school located in a rural county school district. Marlene became interested in whole language while attending a mandatory in-service program sponsored by the district designed to assist kindergarten teachers in rewriting the kindergarten curriculum. The in-service course was taught by instructors from a nearby university and presented information on whole language instruction. Marlene thought she might like to try some ideas presented in the course and was also interested in using learning centers to "teach" concepts. Again, a teacher educator agreed to offer support and assistance in helping Marlene develop her teaching according to her own goals.

Marlene's Beliefs

1. A teacher needs to be in control of the classroom.

2. Teaching is telling ("stand-up teaching" is the most important kind of teaching).

3. Children need a balance between work and play. "Recent changes in our curriculum are making it harder to find time for the children to play."

4. The state and our district have mandated "all these skills" we must teach to the children.

5. Young children aren't ready to write. "Their little muscles aren't developed yet. I wait until the end of the year to teach handwriting, but their work is still not very good."

6. The phonics program we use is good because "it does not require the children to write, simply to circle and underline."

7. "I really would like to make some changes in my teaching to allow children more time to play, but I don't see how I can do that and meet all the requirements."

Marlene was able to create a kindergarten program that included room for all of her conflicting beliefs. She organized a teacher-led instructional period in the morning in which she would introduce basic concepts such as colors, shapes, and numbers through stories and songs. (The skills she believed she was required to teach.) The children would then make a teacher-directed craft illustrative of the concept. During the afternoon, Marlene allowed children time to play at various centers including blocks, housekeeping, Legos, puzzles, and small motor games. During this time, she often supervised "fun art activities" such as finger painting and printing. Marlene did not believe children should spend time writing. She chose a phonics program, which she began in January, that required no letter writing. Children worked in required readiness books during the last month of the school year.

Implementations: Getting Started

Marlene established a writing center during the first week of school as part of her eight centers. She set aside a small table, supplied it with paper, crayons, and pencils and laminated a small copy of the ABCs to the tabletop. During each day, two groups of four children would have an opportunity to "work" at the writing center. Although she had "set up the center," she was unsure as to what the children should do: "I just don't know what to do with children this age—their muscles haven't developed yet."

The teacher educator modeled an activity in which children each made a page for a book entitled *The Red Book*, through drawing a picture of their favorite red objects and dictating a sentence about this picture. The pictures were then stapled together along with a cover and children's names written as authors on the title page. During the following week, Marlene continued the activity with other groups of children and published blue, green, and yellow books with them. These books were kept in the writing center and read by the children. During the few weeks that followed, the children had the opportunity to visit the center and often used the time to draw pictures. Marlene helped the children learn to write their names.

After three weeks, Marlene expressed frustration with her ability to "teach" at the center. She stated she still was unsure what the children should do. The teacher educator restated the purpose of the center: to get kids to express themselves through any kind of written work. Marlene appeared to need this re-explanation at this time. Besides explanations, Marlene also needed specific information on how to handle materials in the center. At first, paper was stacked in the middle of the table. Some children would make a few marks on a sheet and put it back. Those who followed did not like to use previously marked paper. Marlene was shown a way to organize the center. Paper was stored in tagboard pockets hung on an adjacent wall. Children's work was also placed around the center for others to see. Pictures of Halloween characters, added to elicit Halloween stories, motivated the first invented spelling, "GRVB" (the ghosts will say boo). With supplies arranged in a more systematic manner, children began to settle in to work more easily.

Marlene further worried about helping children with their "writing." It was suggested that during cleanup time, she move to the center and take dictation from the writers. As a result, the children came to expect that as their turn in the center ended, Marlene would ask them to dictate to her. By the end of October, Marlene was pleased with the center's operations and her children's learning. "They are no longer happy to just draw a picture. They want you to write those words." By November, Marlene stated, "I'm beginning to see the progress the children are making in perceiving that what they have said can be written down and they can read it."

Initially, Marlene was concerned that the children were not "ready" to write. She did not want to push their "small fingers" into extended writing tasks. As the children continued to work in the center, Marlene commented not only on their learning but also on the fact that "they are happy to be there."

By mid-November, several children moved from drawing pictures to writing letters. Some copied words they saw in the classroom. They would bring their papers to Marlene and reread the words to her. Marlene accepted these rereadings with enthusiasm. One day Scott attempted to make an Indian book. After drawing several pictures, he proudly wrote on the cover "IDNS." Marlene was excited, "I know he'll be reading soon," she exclaimed.

Marlene also began to involve her children much more in listening to storybooks. The teacher educator modeled reading stories in which children repeated predictable text. She also wrote simple books for children on Halloween and on Indians, which the children could "easily" read. These were placed in the library corner and read daily by the children. On one occasion, the Indian books were smuggled into the block corner and shared by two "illegal" readers.

Marlene added a daily experience chart, which she called "Today's News," to her morning routine. Each day, she would write "Today is (day, date, year). It is (weather word). We will make a (name of art project)." This was reread by the children several times during the morning opening. Marlene added simple illustrations to depict the weather and the daily art projects. She stapled a week's worth of "news" to make a book. These books were placed in the writing center and avidly reread, especially the book illustrating the Halloween art projects.

Marlene also began to use experience charts in her morning presentations. She wrote stories about bears hibernating and birds migrating as the children watched. Two categorization charts were developed, one showing the names of children living in different kinds of houses (one-story house, apartment house, and trailer), another chart classifying the kinds of pets children had at home or wished they might have. By December, Marlene was feeling she had made a good start, "I don't know what to expect of my children in this area by the end of the year, but I hope they will be excited about books and reading and writing and will begin to write their own stories."

Problems and Concerns

Marlene believed the writing center worked well in her classroom. She was particularly displeased with her previous method of teaching handwriting during the final month of the year, but her belief in the children's general lack of maturity prevented her from doing so earlier. She was initially unsure if her children would be "able" to write in a writing center but was very much pleased with their learning and also with the fact that they enjoyed the writing center. As the children developed, Marlene was able to restructure her formation to one of children's expression of meaning.

Marlene was eager to try new teaching strategies. However, she requested modeling before she began herself to try a new kind of learning experience. She seemed to need to see "how" in terms of procedural knowledge to place activities into classroom usage. Once she observed a strategy, she would try it out and even innovate on it in subsequent lessons.

However, during this period, Marlene became increasingly frustrated with her teaching during center time. Marlene had decided to "teach more through centers" during this year. In addition to implementing the writing center, the researcher also helped Marlene develop a math center in which children engaged in various classifying and counting activities. Marlene added these two learning centers into her routine of play centers.

The addition of the "learning centers" caused her problems. Marlene defined teaching as direct instruction. She initially did not see how she could "teach" at one center and keep an eye on all the other activities. "It's hard to teach in a center. I just feel that if I'm not in one center, that's it. I can go check to see what someone is doing, but I can't instruct." During the course of their working together, the teacher educator modeled a "facilitative style of teaching" in which she moved from center to center. She also talked to Marlene about defining teaching as working with children through casual interactions. Marlene stated that as she began to try moving from center-to-center rather than conducting a lesson, she could "relax and enjoy the children more." Marlene tended to spend time in the art or the math center, while the children played or wrote in other centers. As the year progressed, she would easily accept children coming to her from the writing center to request dictation or to read their writing to her. This expanded definition of teaching empowered Marlene to teach in a way more congruent with her beliefs about young children.

Summary

Marlene was able to engage her children in reading and writing experiences during the first three months of school. However, she believed she could not make further changes in her program. She stated she felt compelled to teach the skills. In fact, she concurrently was attending a required building in-service program in which she was being taught to write her lesson plans in terms of child performance objectives. She was required to label each of her lesson plans with the appropriate state-specified learning goals. Apparently, these outside influences supported Marlene's beliefs that specific skills needed to be taught separately. Marlene also believed she needed to keep her phonics program so that children would have exposure to all the letters and sounds. She believed this was necessary for children to pass the standardized tests she had to give each May. Nevertheless, she continued to use "Today's News" and experience charts with her children during the morning and encouraged children's efforts at the writing center during the afternoon. She no longer viewed this type of work as "pushing paper and pencil work" on young children but saw it as an appropriate way to begin to work toward developing writing ability with her children.

IMPLICATIONS FOR TEACHER EDUCATION

These stories have presented two individual teachers at various stages in developing a whole language program. Although each story is unique and cannot be generalized to other kindergarten teachers, several implications can be drawn about the process of empowering teachers to develop whole language programs.

It seems reasonable to describe the process of implementing a whole language program as a developmental process. Duffy and Roehler's model (1989) provides a useful heuristic in each of these cases. That is, Sandra, who appeared to have made the most complete implementation of the two, began already firmly grounded in a conceptual and a procedural understanding of how to implement whole language curricular changes. Sandra needed most help in mediating the program, adapting her responses and subsequent instruction to her "problem" students' work.

Marlene grew in conceptual understanding of whole language. She now viewed the process of children learning to write from a meaning-based perspective as well as teaching as including facilitation of learning. She further developed routines that allowed her to place these changing beliefs into classroom practice.

Furthermore, even a limited engagement in whole language activities appears to have an important effect on children's learning. Although Marlene made small steps in implementing a whole language program, the children learned considerably from these experiences and grew in their ability to see themselves as readers and writers (Bruneau, 1988). It would appear helpful to view curricular change as a long process, with important steps made along the way.

A second implication appears to be the powerful effect that modeling had in helping teachers begin to make changes in their curriculum. Marlene needed modeling the most as she began to implement new writing and reading activities. From observing the teacher educator teach and subsequently talking about the lessons, Marlene gained the knowledge and confidence to try new teaching strategies. Sandra, who knew what she wanted to do and how to do it, asked to have lessons modeled during the period she was frustrated in eliciting invented spelling. For both teachers at some time, talking about their teaching did not appear to be enough. They both asked to see new kinds of lessons demonstrated within their classrooms.

A third implication for developing whole language programs appears to be the need to consider the context in which teachers must work. Marlene sincerely wished to develop more integrated experiences for her students; however, she was simultaneously required to specify explicitly learning objectives for each of their lessons. The mandatory school environment pulled her away from what she wanted to do. Sandra operated in a highly supportive school environment. However, the pressure from the "outside world" of expectations of neighboring elementary schools and parental concerns about their children meeting these expectations created self-doubts as to whether she was indeed doing the best she could for her students.

A fourth implication for empowering teachers to develop whole language programs appears to be the need for continual support during the change process. Both teachers needed differing kinds of help at different times. Marlene needed specific information on how to begin. Sandra needed assistance in helping her view growth in her children's work and plan learning experiences for these individual children. Each teacher needed individual information during specific periods of her curricular development. Having their own learning needs met, the teachers were able to continue within their own unique process of development.

Current research on teacher development is beginning to emphasize the individual nature of teacher growth. Wildman and Niles (1987) have suggested a starting point for teacher development that begins with understanding each teacher as a unique learner. A whole language approach to literacy learning suggests teachers focus on the knowledge of written language constructed by each of their students and build learning experiences from this point. A parallel approach toward teacher development suggests teacher educators need to begin through focusing on individual teacher's beliefs and knowledge of teaching as a starting point in empowering teachers to develop their own whole language programs.

REFERENCES

Bolin, F. S. "Reassessment and Renewal in Teaching." In F. A. Bolin and J. M. Falk (Eds.), *Teacher Renewal: Professional Issues, Personal Choices* (pp. 6-16). New York: Columbia University Teachers College Press, 1987.

Bruneau, B. J. "A Case Study of the Process of Reflective Coaching in Collaboration With Teachers in the Process of Planning and Implementing Emergent Literacy Concepts in Their Kindergarten Programs." Unpublished doctoral dissertation. Blacksburg, Virginia: Virginia Tech, 1988.

Bruneau, B. J. and Ambrose, R. P. "Kindergarten and Primary Teachers' Perceptions of Whole Language Instructions." A paper presented at the Annual Meeting of the National Reading Conference, Austin, Texas, December 1989.

Bruneau, B. J., Rasinski, T. V., and Ambrose, R. P. "Parents' Perceptions of Children's Reading and Writing Development in a Whole Language Kindergarten Program." A paper presented at the Annual Meeting of the National Reading Conference, Austin, Texas, December 1989.

Duffy, G. G. and Roehler, L .R. "The Tension Between Information Giving and Mediation: New Perspectives on Instructional Explanation and Teacher Change." In J. Brophy (Ed.), *Advances in Research on Teaching.* New York: JAI Press, Inc., 1989.

Erickson, F. "Qualitative Methods in Research on Teaching." In M. C. Wittrock (Ed.), *Handbook of Research on Teaching* (3rd ed.) (pp. 119-61). New York: Macmillan Publishing Co., 1986.

Falk, J.M. "For Teachers: A Dedication to Reassessment and Renewal." In F.S. Bolin and J. M. Falk (Eds.), *Teacher Renewal: Professional Issues, Personal Choices* (pp. 17-29). New York: Columbia University Teachers College Press, 1987.

Fieman-Nemser, S. and Floden, R. "The Cultures of Teaching." In M. C. Wittrock (Ed.), *Handbook of Research on Teaching* (3rd ed.) (pp. 505-26). New York: Macmillan Publishing Co., 1986.

Harste, J. C., Woodward, V. A. and Burke, C. L. *Language Encounters and Literacy Lessons*. Portsmouth, New Hampshire: Heinemann, 1984.

Joyce, B., Hersh, R., and McKibbin, M. *The Structure of School Improvement.* New York: Longman, Inc., 1983.

Spradley, J. *The Ethnographic Interview*. New York: Holt, Rinehart, and Winston, 1979.

Taylor, N., Blum, I., and Logsdon, D. "The Development of Written Language Awareness: Environmental Aspects and Program Characteristics." *Reading Research Quarterly,* 21 (3), 133-49, 1986.

Teale, W. H. "Emergent Literacy: Reading and Writing Development in Early Childhood." In J. E. Readence and R. S. Baldwin (Eds.), *Thirty-Sixth Yearbook of the National Reading Conference* (pp. 45-74). Rochester, New York: National Reading Conference, 1987.

Teale, W. H. and Sulzby, E. "Emergent Literacy as a Perspective for Examining How Young Children Become Writers and Readers." In W.H. Teale and E. Sulzby (Eds.), *Emergent Literacy: Writing and Reading* (pp. vii-xxv). Norwood, New Jersey: Ablex, 1986.

Wildman, T. M. and Niles, J. A. "Essentials of Professional Growth." *Educational Leadership*, 44, 4-10, 1987.

Beverly J. Bruneau is a faculty member at Kent State University.

JAMES ZARRILLO

Empowered Teachers and Children
WHAT STUDENTS READ IN A WHOLE LANGUAGE CLASSROOM

During the last three years I have spent time in many elementary classrooms researching literature-based reading programs (Cox and Zarrillo, 1990; Zarrillo, 1988; Zarrillo, 1989). Though several of the teachers I observed continued to teach with literature as they did when using basal readers, others were committed to a literacy program consistent with the whole language philosophy. As my investigations proceeded, I came to the conclusion that an important issue for whole language teachers is how they share decision-making responsibilities with students, especially in the selection of the material students read. In this article I will place this issue in historical perspective, review the current situation in elementary schools, discuss the collaborative and democratic nature of whole language classrooms, and share two success stories from my research.

WHAT STUDENTS READ:
A HISTORICAL PERSPECTIVE

Perhaps Dewey summarized it best when he wrote, "The history of educational theory is marked by opposition between the idea that education is development from within and that it is formation from without" (1938, p.17). Indeed, the question of who will determine the child's curriculum is an ancient one, garnering the attention of philosophers from Plato to the present. Those who would impose a reading curriculum on children have dominated literacy education in the United States (Shannon, 1988; Smith, 1965; Smith, 1986).

There have been, however, two distinct periods when children were permitted to play a significant role in selecting what they read in school. The progressives of the late nineteenth and early twentieth century attempted to bring the child to the center of the educational experience (Cremin, 1962). Contemporary teachers seeking to create whole language classrooms should consider the inspiration of Col. Francis W. Parker (1883, 1894). As superintendent of the Quincy, Massachusetts, schools in the 1870s and as principal of the Cook County Normal School in Chicago in the 1880s and 1890s, Parker abandoned reading texts as students wrote their own reading materials. Reading, writing, and the arts were seen "as vehicles for child expression, all began with what had meaning to the children themselves" (Cremin, 1962, p. 133). In the most prominent progressive school, Dewey's University of Chicago Laboratory School, children had considerable, but not unlimited, freedom to decide what they would read and write. In fact descriptions of the educational program at the Laboratory School still provide some of the finest examples of teaching and learning based on thematic units (Dewey, 1897; Mayhew & Edwards, 1936). Parker and Dewey considered books and the ability to read as tools for learning about subject matter. Within areas of study, children were encouraged to pursue individual topics of inquiry. Textbooks were replaced with literature and written work produced by children. Thus, to an extent unequalled in American schools until that time, children in progressive classrooms could select their reading material.

The second period of student empowerment occurred in the 1950s and 1960s. Willard Olson's 1949 work on individual differences served as a framework for the development of self-selection, self-pacing reading programs. "Individualized Reading" became the generic descriptor of classrooms where children selected material of personal interest and conferenced periodically with their teacher (Veatch, 1959). Though thousands of teachers tried Individualized Reading, their numbers never grew to more than 5 percent of all elementary teachers in the United States, and it is difficult to make generalizations about them. Certainly they maximized student responsibility in the selection of reading material. Though studies comparing one instructional approach to another must be viewed with considerable caution, children in Individualized Reading programs usually performed better on standardized reading tests than comparable groups of students in basal reading programs (Krashen, 1985). Despite this success, Individualized Reading was driven from the schools by forces (publishers of basals, academics who wrote them, and school administrators) interested in maintaining control over teachers, students, and the curriculum (Veatch, 1986).

I recommend Yetta Goodman's excellent discussion of the historical and philosophical roots of whole language (1989), including the influences of progressive education and Individualized Reading, to readers who want to learn more about this topic.

WHAT STUDENTS READ:
THE CURRENT SITUATION

An essential tenet of the whole language philosophy is that classrooms become democratic, that teachers delegate considerable responsibility to students in determining what they read and write, and that teachers and students have a collaborative relationship (Altwerger, Edelsky and Flores, 1977; Goodman, 1986). Student choice is essential in order for classroom practice to be consistent with the theories of learning and language development that serve as the foundation for whole language. Shannon argues that political and sociological factors also provide a rationale for giving students the power to decide what they read (1989).

It is somewhat ironic that at the same time the whole language philosophy is giving children greater control over what they read, other forces are establishing canons of children's books that impose a literature curriculum on teachers and students. Hirsch has argued that there is a body of knowledge that every American needs to know, and to be culturally literate all students should read a common set of books (1987). Ravitch and Finn decry the lack of knowledge of literature demonstrated by American adolescents and believe that all students be required to read works that are part of a shared American heritage (1987). (Whether or not such constructs as "cultural literacy" and "shared American heritage" exist, and if they do, what purposes they serve, is beyond the scope of this article.) Others, with a desire to connect children with good books, argue that all children should read the best of children's literature.

The result has been the creation of core curricula required of all students. Perhaps the most influential list is the California State Department of Education's *Recommended Readings in Literature: Kindergarten Through Grade Eight* (1986). *Recommended Readings* established a list of 227 core books that must "be taught in the classroom [and] given close reading and intensive consideration" (p. ix). School districts assign the core books to grade levels, and students and teachers, to borrow Aidan Chambers's phrasing, "plod through them in a kind of literary pilgrimage" (1983, p. 75).

We are in contradictory times, then, in regard to who will decide what children read in elementary classrooms. A large number of teachers continue to use basal readers. Shannon discussed how the new, mislabeled "whole language basals" disenfranchise both students and teachers, just as skills-oriented and interactionist basals do (1987). Student control over reading material is limited to selection of books for brief silent reading periods that are an impoverished stepchild of the activities dictated by the basal program. Other classrooms are literature-based in that books have replaced the basals, but either a state agency, a district committee, or the classroom teacher has mandated a literature curriculum with a list of required readings. Students spend September reading *Island of the Blue Dolphins,* October with *Stuart Little,* November with *The Indian in the Cupboard,* and on through the months of the school year, ten pages a day. As in basal classrooms, student selection of reading material is restricted to choice of a book for reading after the completion of required follow-up assignments to the core books.

WHAT STUDENTS READ:
COLLABORATION AND DEMOCRACY

No two whole language classrooms are alike. When it came to deciding what students would read, I observed teachers and students collaborating in a variety of productive ways. Two points should be stressed:

1. Children are at the center of the whole language classroom. A high level of student decision making is essential if students are to develop fully as readers and writers. If children are to use language as it should be used—for communicative purposes—then children must play the major role in determining what they read and write. Children will learn to read with less pain, at an earlier point, and with greater frequency in settings where their reading interests are respected (see, for example, Bissex, 1980; Clark, 1976; Cyrog, 1962; Duker, 1968; Durkin, 1966; Morrow and Weinstein, 1986).

2. Teachers will continue to influence what students read in the whole language classroom. There are many misconceptions about whole language. Consider the comments one teacher made to me at a district in-service: "I'm not ready to abandon ship and let kids do whatever they want; that's anarchy, and so whole language isn't for me." This teacher's perception was unduly influenced by a colleague who was preoccupied with torpedoing the reforms that were sweeping her district. Yet I wasn't surprised at her feelings. After being rendered powerless by basal programs that choreograph every move by teacher and student (Shannon, 1987), even a small shift of control may seem apocalyptic and threatening. To set the record straight, teachers should influence student decisions through the books they read aloud and promote through displays and talks. Teachers should help children locate books by favorite authors, within popular genres, and on interesting topics. Teachers should fulfill their responsibility as caring adults and shield children from adult literature that is clearly inappropriate for young readers.

WHAT STUDENTS READ: TWO SUCCESS STORIES

Among the many students and teachers I observed, two situations served as positive and productive examples of how students can assume responsibility for choosing the material they read in collaboration with their teacher.

Julie and the Newberry Winners. Julie was a fifth-grader with extraordinary ability. Julie's reading tastes were eclectic. She had read and enjoyed three Newberry winners but was spending more and more of her time reading serial novels popular with upper-elementary girls (*Baby Sitters Club, Sweet Valley High*). Julie needed structure in her schooling. She told me she liked it when she could check things off, "so I know what I have finished and what is ahead for me." Her teacher was in the second year of transitioning from basal-oriented instruction to a whole language literacy program. Julie's teacher wanted her students to design yearlong projects that would involve a considerable amount of reading. In October, Julie saw a list of the Newberry Award-winning books and asked her teacher for more information about their selection. Later that week, Julie and her teacher agreed on a project: Julie would read all of the Newberry winners and write a response to each. In May, Julie completed the project, using the school and two public libraries to find all the books. Her written responses are fascinating, showing a strong sense of personal preference, offering criticis , and frequently comparing the books in theme, style, and plot.

Make Way for Readlings. Curtis, Debbie, and Sharon were second-graders with very different interests and abilities. Their teacher, John Potenza, taught in a district that established eight core books for second grade. This meant each child was to have a copy of the book, and the teacher was to devote more than one instructional period to reading and follow-up activities. Though Mr. Potenza considered this curricular mandate to be inconsistent with the democratic nature of his whole language classroom and his self-selection reading and writing program, he was able to use the core books in a manner consistent with his way of teaching. In February, it was his turn to use Robert McCloskey's *Make Way for Ducklings* (teachers shared the 35 paperback copies of each core book on a rotating basis). Mr. Potenza read *Make Way* aloud. Afterwards he asked his students "to write and draw whatever you want about this story." The next day he asked children to read to each other their favorite parts, and then children shared their favorite illustrations.

Afterwards, it was time for independent reading and writing and individual conferences with Mr. Potenza. He met with three children that day, each pursuing a different reading course following *Make Way for Ducklings*. Mr. Potenza had displayed copies of other McCloskey books in the reading corner. Curtis, the first student to meet with Mr. Potenza, decided he would like to read the books on display, and returned to his seat with *One Morning in Maine*. Mr. Potenza met next with Sharon, whose mother was a police officer. They chatted about Michael, the corpulent cop in *Make Way for Ducklings*. Sharon noted that Michael didn't wear the same type of uniform as her mother and that he didn't carry a gun. Mr. Potenza suggested Sharon go to the school library with a sixth-grade helper and find some books that show how police officers have dressed over the last one hundred years. Sharon said she would like to draw some pictures of different uniforms, and Mr. Potenza agreed. Debbie, the next child to come up for a conference, was enthusiastically reading Norman Bridwell's *Clifford* books. The conference consisted of Debbie talking nonstop about Clifford. Mr. Potenza brought up *Make Way for Ducklings* and showed Debbie the nonfiction books on ducks he had brought to class, suggesting that she might want to find out more about how ducks live. Debbie wasn't interested. Mr. Potenza wished her luck with *Clifford at the Circus*.

WHAT STUDENTS READ:
EMPOWERED TEACHERS AND CHILDREN

In the whole language classroom teachers and students are empowered. In democratic and collaborative whole language classrooms teachers and children journey together through the worlds of children's books. Teachers are freed of the constraints of basal reading programs. The choice of which books to emphasize and promote should be left to teachers, and implementation of core literature curricula should be reconsidered. In whole language classrooms teachers will continue to influence the reading decisions of their students, but children will assume responsibility for what they read. After all, the empowered child is the easiest to teach, the most likely to develop as a literate being.

REFERENCES

Altwerger, B., Edelsky, C. and Flores, B.M. "Whole Language: What's New." *The Reading Teacher*, 41, pp.144-155, 1987.

Bissex, G. L. *GNYS AT WRK: A Child Learns to Read and Write.* Cambridge, Massachusetts: Harvard University Press, 1980.

Chambers, A. *Introducing Books to Children.* Boston: The Horn Book, 1983.

Clark, M. M. *Young Fluent Readers: What Do They Teach Us?* London: Heinemann, 1976.

Cox, C. and Zarrillo, J. "Teaching with Literature in the Elementary school: A Qualitative Study Applying Rosenblatt's Transactional Theory." Paper presented at the meeting of the American Educational Research Association, Boston, April 1990.

Cremin, L. *The Transformation of the School.* New York: Alfred Knopf, 1962.

Cyrog, F. C. "Self-selection in reading: Report of a Longitudinal Study." In M.P. Douglass (Ed.), Claremont Reading Conference Twenty-Sixth Yearbook, pp. 106-113. Claremont, California: Claremont Reading Conference.

Dewey, J. "The University Elementary School: History and Character." *University Record,* 2, 72-75. Also available in J. A. Boydston (Ed.), John Dewey: *The Middle Works,* 1899-1924, Volume 1: 1899-1901, pp. 325-334. Carbondale, Illinois: Southern Illinois University Press. 1987.

Dewey, J. *Experience and Education.* New York: Macmillan. 1938.

Douglass, M. P. *Learning to Read: The Quest for Meaning.* New York: Teachers College Press, 1989.

Duker, S. *Individualized Reading: An Annotated Bibliography.* Metuchen, New Jersey: The Scarecrow Press, 1968.

Durkin, D. *Children Who Read Early: Two Longitudinal Studies.* New York: Teachers College Press, 1966.

Goodman, K. *What's Whole in Whole Language?* Portsmouth, New Hampshire: Heinemann, 1986.

Goodman, Y. "The Roots of Whole Language." *The Elementary School Journal,* 89, 1989. 90, pp. 113-127.

Hirsch, E. D. *Cultural Literacy: What Every American Needs to Know.* Boston: Houghton Mifflin, 1987.

Krashen, S. *Inquiries and Insights.* Hayward, California: Alemany Press, 1985.

Mayhew, K. C. and Edwards, A. C. *The Dewey School: The Laboratory School of the University of Chicago 1896-1903.* New York: D. Appleton-Century, 1986.

Morrow, L. M. and Weinstein, C. S. "Encouraging Voluntary Reading: The Impact of a Literature Program on Children's Use of Library Centers." *Reading Research Quarterly,* 21, pp. 330-346, 1986.

Olson, W. E. *Child Development.* Boston: D.C. Heath, 1949.

Parker, F. W. *Talks on Teaching.* New York: E.L. Kellogg, 1883.

Parker, F. W. *Talks on Pedagogics.* New York: E.L. Kellogg, 1894.

Ravitch, D. and Finn, C. E. *What Do Our 17-year Olds Know? A Report on the First National Assessment of History and Literature.* New York: Harper & Row, 1987.

Recommended Readings in Literature: Kindergarten Through Grade Eight. Sacramento: California State Department of Education, 1986.

Shannon, P. "Commercial Reading Materials, A Technological Ideology, and the Deskilling of Teachers." *The Elementary School Journal,* 87, pp. 307-329, 1987.

Shannon, P. *Broken Promises: Reading Instruction In 20th Century America.* Granby, Massachusetts: Bergin & Garvey, 1988.

Shannon, P. "The Struggle for Control of Literacy Lessons." *Language Arts,* 66, pp. 625-634, 1989.

Smith, F. *Insult to Intelligence: The Bureaucratic Invasion of Classrooms.* Portsmouth, New Hampshire: Heinemann, 1986.

Smith, N. B. *American Reading Instruction.* Newark, Delaware: International Reading Association, 1965.

Veatch, J. (Ed.) *Individualizing Your Reading Program: Self-Selection in Action.* New York: G.P. Putnam's Sons, 1959.

Veatch, J. "Individualized Reading: A Personal Memoir." *Language Arts,* 63, pp. 586-593, 1986.

Zarrillo, J. "Literature-Centered Reading Programs in Elementary Classrooms." *Dissertation Abstracts International,* 49, 1366A. University Microfilms No. 8811932, 1989.

Zarrillo, J. "Teachers' Interpretations of Literature-Based Reading." *The Reading Teacher,* 43, pp. 22-28, 1989.

James Zarillo is a faculty member at California State University, Long Beach.

JOYCE E. MANY

The Music of Literature
LET STUDENTS CREATE THEIR OWN RENDITION

> The text of a poem or a novel or a drama is like a musical score. The artist who created the score—composer or poet—has set down notations for others, to guide them in the production of the work of art....Moreover, in the literary reading, even the keyboard on which the performer plays is—himself. From the linkage of his own experiences with words, from his own store of memories, he must draw the appropriate elements symbolized by the score of text, to structure a new experience, the work of art.
>
> *Rosenblatt, 1978, p.13*

In the above quote, Rosenblatt reminds us that each student's experience with a literary work is a unique event. Every student will play the piece differently, creating a story world that is part of him or her, building on the foundation laid out in the marks on the page. In the same way, responses to the same story will be as unique as the individual students who make them, just as the responses of audience members listening to a concert will vary.

PERSONAL UNDERSTANDING

One way students' experiences with literature will vary will be in the personal understandings drawn from the works they read. The advent of the reader response movement has meant a new valuing of the self-knowledge and understanding of others, which can be gained through literary transactions (Cooper, 1985). Consequently, reader-response theory can provide a theoretical base for whole language teachers who believe in empowering their students during the literary experience. Instead of expecting students to read a selection and come up with the theme or answer in the teacher's manual, teachers provide students with the freedom to seek for understandings that have personal significance and relevance.

To demonstrate the capabilities of young students in terms of arriving at individual understandings from literary works, let us examine the responses of some upper-elementary and middle school students when asked to "write anything you want about the story you just read" (Many, 1989). That personal understanding has been drawn is evident in responses that break out of the confines of the text and examine the story in terms of the world horizon of the reader. This is apparent in the following response by Johnny, a fourth-grader, to "The Runaway" (Holman, 1976), a short story about a young girl who feels smothered by her parents' love and decides to run away.

> This is a good story to read because it talks about how people feel and how people treat them sometimes. And running away is not the sloution [solution] for that. I think that you should talk to your parents about that.
> *Johnny, grade 4*

Johnny had come away from the reading experience with his own perception of how to solve a similar problem in real life, in his own world. His response is not necessarily centered on what might be considered "the theme" of the story but instead centers on what is useful and significant to him, at this time, as a result of his unique transaction with the text.

At times story events strike a particularly personal chord in readers, such as found in the next two responses to the same story.

> I think this story was very realistic. I can defanatly [definitely] relate to this girls problems. This happes [happens] to me alot. I've almost run away once, because I felt crowded. So this story is a really good one to me because it's so down to earth. I liked the fact that she had a pushy friend because I have one too. This was a neat story because it was full of realistic stuff and it

sort of relates to my everyday life. It is what I want in a story. I have many times planed how to escape or runaway, and I like her because she had some wild ideas. Sometimes I think up wild stuff but then I alwase [always] come back to square one, reality. I like the way that she felt croweded [crowded] in. I sometimes have this feeling. I think this was a real good story and I wouldnt mind reading it again."

Jenny, grade 6

It was kind of instering [interesting]. I mean it was also stupid. I would have killed anybody if they bit me on the leg for no reason. And that chick is going to cry when she runs away! When I ran I was happy. Plus going over to a friends house. NO WAY! Man [that] ain't gonna help yo [you] out none. Pluse [plus] She don't know what trouble is. I been living away from my house for 3 1/3 years. For running, stealing, doing drugs, trespazing [trespassing] and vandializing [vandalizing]. She had no reason to go away from home. It was not realistic in some ways. Well there you have it.

Stan, grade 8

Both students made strong autobiographical connections to the events in the story. In the case of Jenny, the story rang true, mirroring her own experiential background. She recognizes herself, her friends, and episodes of her life experiences as similar to those of the characters. In contrast, while Stan also can relate to the subject presented, he eventually rejects the story world as not being true to his version of reality. Whether acceptance or rejection of the story world has occurred, however, both students have been exposed to a glimpse of possibilities offered from the world horizon of the author with which to compare to their own understanding about life.

Some students go beyond considering specific events from the story world and are able to come away with a more abstract generalization about life. Take for example the two responses below, which attempt to put into words students' understanding of a "moral" for the story "Secret of the Aztec Idol" (Bonham, 1976).

I like it a lot. It has a moral in it, don't take something

that you know is wrong, I like the part were [where] the boy got the idol.

Alicia, grade 4

I think that the story was an excellent story, and it had a very good moral to it. I think the story's moral was, always have proof before you believe. It was really awesome dood [dude].

Tom, grade 6

In both cases, students have gone beyond specific events in the story to deduce what is, for them, something to be remembered. Both morals are valid in terms of the story world, but more importantly each student's rendition of the story is significant in that it was the result of the student's personal attempt to find meaning in what had been read.

While there is evidence that fourth-graders are capable of applying story events to life and reaching abstract generalizations in their free responses to what they have read, the ability to do so does seem to increase significantly at the sixth- and eighth-grade levels (Many, 1989). The following response by an eighth-grader illustrates the complexity that responses can reach when students are allowed to respond freely as they consider what they have read. Victoria is writing about Werner's (1979) "The Dollar's Worth," a short story about a young girl's encounter with prejudice as she works at a gas station.

This was a good story. It showed two different sides of people. It showed how the man really felt and how he had to act. Some people don't understand those two sides. You don't really have to know someone just look at how they act. If someone acts hyper or shows off, they may not be doing it just because they want to, but probably because they want some attention.

This man in the story, Mr. Watts, probably wasn't really a mean man, he just wanted someone to talk to or he was just defending himself so people wouldn't feel sorry for him. Maybe he didn't want anyone to know he was poor, because he might have felt ashamed. He also might not really have been prejudice against girls but maybe something bad happened, that a girl did to him. He might have even wanted to marry some girl and they

wouldn't. But you can't really be angry with people like
that, because if you are a person you should know how
people act.

Victoria, grade 8

Victoria has articulated her beliefs about people and what they are
like. She mulls over how individuals might act differently from the way they
really feel and underscores that underlying motives or past experiences can
influence how people deal with specific situations. In a classroom situation
where student responses were guided by questions from a teacher's guide,
or even by thoughtful questions from the teacher, such individual personal
interaction and meaning making might not take place. By allowing students
first to transact with the text as distinct individuals and then to respond to it
by attending to those features that are personally significant, we can open up
to students a world of literature that is uniquely meaningful to them.

READER STANCE

When teachers wish to encourage students to reach their own
personal understandings from the literary works they read, it is important
to consider factors that might influence students' understanding of and
response to text. One such factor is their focus of attention or stance while
reading or responding (Rosenblatt, 1978, 1985; Cox & Many, 1989; Many, in
press, 1989). According to Rosenblatt, a reader's stance can range from
primarily aesthetic to primarily efferent. When students assume an aesthetic stance, they attend to the lived-through experience of the story and
the thoughts, feelings, and images that the story evokes. When reading from
an efferent stance, on the other hand, students pay attention to the information to be learned in the reading event. The text is studied or analyzed and
the reader attempts to retain that which he/she considers important to
know.

To clarify by referring again to our musical analogy, consider the
following: "A young girl is sitting by herself at a musical concert. Staring into
space, she is transported by the melody into a world of her own." This
member of the audience is listening from an aesthetic stance. She is focusing
on the musical experience and savoring the thoughts, associations, emo-
tions, and ideas that are evoked. In the classroom, however, students rarely
enjoy the unrestricted freedom when reading and responding to literature
that they do when they are playing music or enjoying a concert. Teachers,

in an effort to encourage comprehension, understanding, or vocabulary growth, often wield great power over students' literary experiences and their responses to those experiences. Students are expected to be able to answer questions immediately after or during reading, to summarize, analyze, and interpret. One can hardly imagine being given a pop quiz after attending a symphony, or being asked to recall what notes the cello played immediately before the last crescendo. But unlike music, film, or theater, literature is often taken out of the realm of the literary work of art and is treated as a reading text.

When students do focus on the aesthetic stance, on the lived-through experience of the story, creative and imaginative things happen. Students visualize settings and characters, they place themselves in characters' shoes, they hypothesize alternative endings. This is poignantly visible in the following response to the short story "The Runaway." An eighth-grade student, Amy, chose to form her evocation to the story as a poem, stepping into the main character, Marcia's, shoes and writing from what she conjectures as Marcia's voice.

> I'm Marcia
> Everyone's ideal
> Their precious darling
> Their perfect angel.
> Yet through the superficial smile
> The false, gay smile,
> The golden hair,
> The dreamy skin,
> The angelic features,
> I am dead.
> Emotionally dead.
> I've died many times before my death,
> With all the oohing and ahing they
> never really seemed to care.
> Now a razor blade shall end it all,
> and they might take notice
> And I'll be equal
> And a dead silence will bring
> the oohs and ahs to
> a sudden and lifeless
> halt.
>   *Amy, grade 8*

Amy's almost shocking response carries her far beyond the story world offered by the author. She becomes so entranced with Marcia that she continues on, weaving imagined events and feelings into her own melodramatic ending. This creative work is a result of Amy feeling free to choose not only the content of her response, but the form as well. The aesthetic focus is apparent in her deep involvement in the story world, to the point of assuming the persona of the character herself.

Students who respond from an aesthetic stance often suggest ways in which they would change story events or characters, not necessarily as an attempt to improve the literary quality of the work, but because they are so involved in the story itself that they would like to see what might have happened if. Some students suggest how they would have acted if they had been in the characters' shoes or come to a realization that they would have liked a character more if only the character had been a little different. Take, for example, Herbert's vignette, which clarifies the personality he would have liked for the the old fisherman in "The Secret of the Aztec Idol," a mystery about two young boys who get tricked by a con man.

> If the man was as much of a jerk as the man in this story and if the secrets were so dumb, I wouldn't have bought one. That man was so conceited and concerned about himself that I hated him. You could tell from the beginning by the way he talked about welfare, it was the way he said it and what he said about it that made you know he was a jerk. A friendly old guy who enjoyed kids might have had a different approach for selling a secret. He would have been nicer and more interesting. Like an old man who loves to see kids steal peaches off his tree because he likes seeing the kids so joyful and right when the kids got just one peach runs out of his house and shouts, "You rotten little brats! I'll get you for this!" Even though he really doesn't mean it, he just likes to give the kids a good time and make them feel important.
>
> *Herbert, grade 8*

Like all responses written from an aesthetic stance, the focus of Herbert's response is on the story experience and the images and associations evoked as the story was read. The ability to assume this stance is not affected by grade level; fourth-graders are just as capable as eighth-graders at living through what occurs during the reading event. In terms of personal understanding, students who respond to literature from an aesthetic stance are significantly more likely to interpret story events, to apply story events to life, and to make abstract generalizations than are students who focus on an efferent stance (Cox & Many, 1989; Many, in press; Many, 1989).

The efferent stance is apparent when students center their attention on the information to be carried away from the reading event (Rosenblatt, 1978). While this stance is appropriate for informational texts, it also, unfortunately, is often the stance encouraged by teaching strategies used with literature in reading and language-arts classes. This occurs when attention is focused during the reading event to read for a purpose, to find out specific information, or to determine the lesson to be learned. Vocabulary is picked out and discussed in context, word attack skills are introduced and reviewed. Children are expected to identify main characters, to sequence events, or to summarize the plot. While such activities may indeed be worthwhile activities, they can also lead children to believe that the reason for reading literature is to find out information and that the appropriate thing to do while reading stories is to analyze what is being read.

Rosenblatt (1982) contends that when children do attempt to analyze literary works, the result is often shallow responses. This is illustrated in the free responses below, written from an efferent stance.

> I like the story. I liked the setting and plot. The end was great. The place and time is OK. I like Charlie and Brian.
>
> *Caleb, grade 4, "The Secret of the Aztec Idol"*

> I think it was a good story. I like how it was a mystery and how it was easy to understand. The plot was real good, so was the setting. I liked everything about this story.
>
> *Jacob, grade 8, "The Secret of the Aztec Idol"*

This is not to say that children should never learn the literary elements or be encouraged to be aware of literary quality in the works they read. But instead of analytically distancing themselves from the text, students should be encouraged first to focus on the story experience itself and then to analyze the work, keeping in mind the richness of the original lived-through experience (Rosenblatt, 1978). This mingling of the aesthetic evocation with the efferent analysis can lead to a much more sophisticated, meaningful response (Many, in press). This is depicted in the response below, where Jim weaves his critique of the author's development of character and setting in with glimpses of the vividness of these elements during his original evocation.

> This story was very good. The author (Herma Werner) did a very good job in giving the characters personality. Just by reading that story, I hate Mr. Watts too. The only thing this story was lacking was a good description of this place. I pictured it out in the country where there isn't much traffic and there aren't many stores. But I don't know. For all I know it could be in New York City. (Except for when it said Mr. Watts went putting along the street at 10 miles per hour.) Other than that, the story was excellent.
>
> *Jim, grade 8, "The Dollar's Worth"*

In closing, be encouraged to open up to children opportunities to focus on and experience the worlds found in books. Value the personal understandings that they reach as they leave the confines of the text and apply the story to life and utilize teaching techniques that encourage them to live through the story experience.

To do this, first be aware of how you are using literature in the classroom. Do not relegate it only to serving as a text for reading/language-arts instruction, or teaching lessons (morality), or even as a vehicle for teaching about plot, setting, or characterization. Allow students the freedom to live in the story, to visualize the images conjured up by the interplay of their own backgrounds and the author's words, to hypothesize and conjecture over "what ifs," and to savor the flavor of the language itself. Support their personal experience of the reading event.

Second, avoid using ping-pong questioning with literature in an effort to monitor or increase student comprehension. Such techniques could give students the impression that the appropriate focus while reading literature is to read to find out information, thus encouraging an efferent stance. In contrast, teaching activities that support the aesthetic stance can result in students reaching greater heights of personal understanding.

Third, remember that children's initial attempts at analyzing the literary elements in books are often trite and shallow. To encourage more complex critiques, first have students read stories and focus on the aesthetic stance (the ideas, feelings, and associations that come to mind as they live the story experience). Then encourage students to evaluate the literature in terms of why it was or was not successful in capturing their interest during their original aesthetic evocation.

Empowering students during the reading experience in such ways allows them to read and freely respond to the world that unfolds between the pages of the book and the pictures they paint for themselves as they experience the reading event. Doing so can provide them insights not only about others but about themselves as well. It frees them up to be creative and imaginative, to experience new worlds and reconsider their own, as they play their own renditions of the beautiful melodies found in literature.

REFERENCES

Bonham, F. "Secret of the Aztec Idol." In A. Diven (Ed.), *The Scribner Anthology for Young People* (pp. 116-124). New York: Charles Scribner's Sons, 1976.

Cooper, C. R. (Ed.) *Researching Response to Literature and the Teaching of Literature.* Norwood, New Jersey: Ablex, 1985.

Cox, C., and Many, J. E. "Reader Stance Towards a Literary Work: Applying the Transactional Theory to Children's Responses." Paper presented at the Annual Meeting of the American Educational Research Association, San Francisco, California, March 1989.

Holman, F. "The Runaway." In A. Diven (Ed.), *The Scribner Anthology for Young People* (pp. 17-21). New York: Charles Scribner's Sons, 1976.

Many, J. E. (in press). "The Effect of Reader Stance on Students' Personal Understanding of Literature." In S. McCormick and J. Zutell (Eds.), *Thirty-eighth Yearbook of the National Reading Conference.*

Many, J. E. "Age Level Differences in Children's Use of an Aesthetic Stance When Responding to Literature." Unpublished dissertation, LouisianaState University, Baton Rouge, Louisiana, 1989.

Rosenblatt, L. M. *The Reader, the Text, the Poem: The Transactional Theory of the Literary Work.* Carbondale, Illinois: Southern Illinois University Press, 1978.

Rosenblatt, L. M. "The Literary Transaction: Evocation and Response." *Theory Into Practice,* 21, 268-277, 1982.

Rosenblatt, L. M. "The Transactional Theory of the Literary Work." In C.R. Cooper (Ed.), *Researching Response to Literature and the Teaching of Literature* (pp. 33-53). Norwood, New Jersey: Ablex, 1985.

Joyce E. Many is a faculty member at Texas A & M University.

CAROLE COX

Making Choices, Gaining Control

A TRANSACTIONAL VIEW OF TEACHING AESTHETICALLY WITH LITERATURE

Nancy Cothern, a teacher in a fifth-grade literature-based class, has asked her students to read *Where the Red Fern Grows*. Nancy does not use a basal reader or a language-arts textbook. She uses novels, poetry, short stories, magazines, newspapers, film, video, and students' own writing as the whole, meaningful texts she believes are most appropriate for the growth and development of literacy and thinking among her students. Her room is littered with paperback books, encyclopedias, reference books, magazines old and new, files of newspaper clippings, and the students' own writing: journals, reports on topics of interest, scripts, and so on. It smells funny. Like a used-book store, an old library, or a house where real readers live—the kind who can't bear to get rid of a book or a magazine that they once read and enjoyed and still remember.

Just as she has made the choice to reject commercial educational materials and choose instead materials that people in the real world really read and use, she gives her students the choice to make decisions about what they read, how they respond to their reading, and what they do about their reading as a result. Nancy is in control of her own program. She has gained this control not by limiting it to one programmed set of materials with a teacher's guide and carefully planned, sequenced, and evaluated activities in a unisex/one-size fits all model, but by expanding her options to include many forms of literariness and by opening the options of her students as well to make decisions about what they do during and after they read. She knows that when students—like teachers—are able to make choices, they also gain control. They gain control of their own situation, experiences, ideas, and, consequently, of their own learning and development as readers, writers, and thinkers.

TWO RESPONSES TO WHERE THE RED FERN GROWS

But what happens in such a room when thirty students read and freely respond to the same book? Here are two of the written responses of children in this class to *Where the Red Fern Grows.*

Adrienne writes:

I like the book *Where the Red Fern Grows* because it made me feel nice. The Ozarks, where Billy lived, seemed just like the perfect place to grow up. It seemed really great. It amazed me that Billy could save his money for two years without giving up or even telling someone what he was doing. I really liked the book because it made me feel like I was on a vacation and had all the time in the world left just for living. It made me feel free. Time just stood still. It was great. I was always sorry when time for reading the book was over in class.

And Geneva writes:

Well first of all, I really did not like *Where the Red Fern Grows* because the author was kind of fiction-like and the plot was not good at all. That's why I don't like *Where the Red Fern Grows,* but some of it I did like.

These are obviously very different responses to the same book. Not very surprising when you give children the opportunity to write what they think. Children are different. Why not their literary responses? But how do teachers who use a literature-based program make sense of such differences?

Among the many current ideas that might inform and empower whole language teachers and students in their classrooms, reader-response criticism such as Rosenblatt's (1978) transactional theory of the literary work offers a means to understand the fascinating differences among students' responses to literature, like those of Adrienne and Geneva to *Where the Red Fern Grows.*

THE TRANSACTIONAL THEORY

Reader-response theories center on the recognition of the very active role of the responder in not only encountering but creating "the literary work." Rosenblatt (1986) calls this "the object of interpretation, appreciation, analysis, criticism, evaluation...the evocation lived through by the reader-critic during the transaction with the text." Much more than passive recipients during an encounter with literary discourse, responders such as Adrienne and Geneva are actively engaged in the process of commingling their own experiences, ideas, feelings, and perceptions with the actual text as written. The text serves as a pattern, guiding the reader through the creation of a personal version of the literary work. What they create is a virtual literary work, or what Rosenblatt has termed the "poem" (1978).

Because readers differ, their experiences during any reading event are also likely to differ. All readers will not focus on the same aspects of a text or find identical points personally meaningful. Rosenblatt (1978) describes a reader's focus of attention as the reader's stance. Stance represents a readiness to organize the reading experience according to a particular framework.

While all reading occurs as experienced meaning, readers may adopt a position that falls on a continuum from a more efferent to a more aesthetic stance. A more efferent reading would focus attention on the information provided in the text or ideas acquired through what is being referred to—the more lexical, public aspects. It is more likely to evolve as a kind of study of the text with an emphasis on breaking it up into isolated segments and concentrating on certain information to be retained according to one or another analytical system or way of viewing it. An aesthetic reading, on the other hand, indicates that the focus of the reader's attention is on the lived-through experience of the work—the more personal, private aspects. It evolves through attention to the individual nature of the experienced meaning and focuses on the selective process of creating a literary work of art through the transaction between the reader and the text.

Reader-response theory has brought about a new conception of the role of the reader in constructing meaning from text. Each reader's evocation of a text is uniquely personal, as are the subsequent interpretations. Ricoeur (1976) describes interpretation as occurring out of a dialectic give-and-take between the world horizon of the author and the world horizon of the reader. The reader's understanding of what something means in the text is expanded to its relevance to other possible worlds (Bruner, 1985). This offers an alternative to the view that readers should primarily aim toward finding an agreed-upon meaning of a text, of correctly interpreting the work's "theme." Instead, readers can experience the work and find meaning in light of their own worlds or any world they might imagine.

Because reader-response theories like Rosenblatt's seem to offer great explanatory power for the role of the individual in learning from literature, Joyce Many and I (Cox & Many 1989) used it as a theoretical framework to analyze the literary responses of the students in Nancy Cothern's fifth-grade literature-based whole language classroom over a year's time.

APPLYING THE TRANSACTIONAL THEORY

Responses to books and films were collected throughout the year in Nancy's classroom. Because she did not use a basal reader or language-arts text, her students had ample time to read and view films and respond to them in writing. We chose nine works of realistic fiction selected on the basis of quality and appropriateness for this age. The four novels were *Summer of the Swans; The Great Gilly Hopkins; Phillip Hall Likes Me, I Reckon Maybe ;* and *Where the Red Fern Grows.* These students also viewed films. Rosenblatt takes an eclectic view of the various forms of literariness and their potential as lived-through experience. She suggests that a literary work of art is "not an object but an event, a lived-through process or experience." (1985). It seemed important, therefore, to understand how response evolves through virtual experiences with film as well as literature, especially since students today live in a world full of stories on film. The five films shown were: *The Case of the Elevator Duck, The Tap Dance Kid, The Fur Coat Club, Very Good Friends,* and *Granny Lives in Galway.*

After each reading or viewing event, students responded in writing to the open-ended prompt "Write anything you want about the book/film you just read/saw." These responses were then holistically analyzed, first according to the stance assumed in each response and then according to the level of understanding reached in each response.

READER STANCE TOWARDS A LITERARY WORK				
EFFERENT				AESTHETIC
1	2	3	4	5
Analysis of Elements According to Outside Structure				Focus on the Lived-through Experience of the Literary Work
	Verbatim Retelling		Selection of Story Events or Characters to Elaborate Preference, Judgement, or Description	
		Portions of Both Efferent Analysis and Aesthetic Experience of Work		

TABLE 1

STANCE, FROM EFFERENT TO AESTHETIC

When responses were analyzed, a five-point continuum emerged with responses at one end indicating the most efferent stance and at the other the most aesthetic stance. Table 1 shows a brief description of each point along the stance continuum, and examples of each follow.

The most efferent responses focused on what was learned or information gained from the reading or viewing, rather than the reading or viewing experience itself. The text was analyzed by breaking it down into parts or by placing it into a category and responding accordingly. Most efferent responses were often characterized by literary-critical analysis, production analysis, or analysis using other standards or systems.

This can be seen in Geneva's response to *Where the Red Fern Grows* cited earlier. She focused her attention on the author, genre, and plot of the story. Other students' efferent responses also focused on the structure of the work or other literary elements such as setting, mood, or characters.

The primarily efferent responses at the next point on the continuum focused on simply retelling the story. These responses were either a straight recounting of the narrative or may also have included a preference or judgment statement, but little continuity existed between such statements and the retelling. In response to the film *The Tap Dance Kid*, for example, Danny writes: "I really liked this movie. I'll tell you about it...." The rest of his response is a straight retelling of the story.

Responses that contained a mix of elements of both the aesthetic evocation and efferent analysis without a primary emphasis on either were placed at the midpoint of the continuum.

Toward the aesthetic end of the continuum, the primarily aesthetic responses were formed around selective attention to specific parts of a work. These responses may have stated a preference, made a judgment of quality or character's behavior, or related an impression about story events or people in the story and then described story sections that elicited those responses. Here the responder is paying selective attention to the story world and relating the story part that drew their attention, as this child does in response to the film *The Fur Coat Club*.

> I thought it was OK. When the things came alive it was stupid. There were plenty of movies I liked better. But it was funny how they ran around playing the game, and at the end listening to that guy and girl talking. I would love to be able to do that with my best friend. But getting locked in a vault was unrealistic.

It is the element of choice that characterizes this type of response most. The responders paid selective attention to the part of the story that attracted their attention, but without elaboration on why or what it was about the part that attracted them.

The most aesthetic responses on the stance continuum showed clear evidence of the lived-through experience. Attention was centered on the evocation—the ideas, scenes, images, associations, or feelings called to mind during the reader's transaction with the text. These responses fell into three groups, characterized as imaging and picturing, relating associations and feelings evoked, and hypothesizing, extending, and retrospecting.

Adrienne's response to *Where the Red Fern Grows* cited earlier is primarily aesthetic. She has clearly focused on the personal, lived-through evocation of the work. Key to the placement of her response is that she has organized it around her evoked feelings. She has expressed wonder at a character's behavior. She has imagined herself in the story setting, and she has hypothesized what she would feel like as a result.

Another child responded aesthetically to *Where the Red Fern Grows* when she wrote, "You could picture his affection for the pups and see his wide, proud, happy eyes." This clearly exemplifies the type of picturing and imaging children did when they responded aesthetically. An example of how they also related associations and feelings evoked is this child's response to the film *Very Good Friends:* "I enjoyed the film even though it depressed me. It was sad to think about a little girl who had so much to live for dying."

Children also reflected on story events or a character's behavior by expressing wonder at something they obviously could not readily imagine in the context of their own life experience, as shown in this response to *Where the Red Fern Grows:* "It amazed me how the boy could save his money for years without giving up or even telling someone what he was doing."

Primarily aesthetic responses such as these both showed an expression of a strongly felt sense of the reality of the lived-through experience of the work and demonstrated a high degree of interpretation as a result of the lived-through evocation or by relating a strong awareness of self during reading or viewing.

LEVELS OF PERSONAL UNDERSTANDING

These levels were determined by the degree to which the understanding demonstrated in the response breaks through the boundaries of

LEVELS OF PERSONAL UNDERSTANDING			
(WORD OF TEXT)			**(APPLIED TO LIFE)**
1	**2**	**3**	**4**
Literal Meaning of Story		Application of Understanding of Specific Events to Self or World	
	Interpretation of Story Events		Generalization of beliefs or understandings of Life or People

TABLE 2

the text and is applied to life, rather than whether or not it matches a "correct" or agreed-upon meaning of the text. Table #2 shows a summary description of each of the levels.

At the first level, responders did not go beyond the literal meaning of the story. While responses may have included feelings, statements of preference, or judgments, there was no interpretation beyond the literal. Geneva's response to *Where the Red Fern Grows* cited earlier is an example.

At the next level, responses indicated some interpretation of specific story events but were not generalized beyond the world of the text. Characteristics of this type of response included making judgments, inferences, or explanations. These responses often contained phrases such as "should have, because, seems like," as in this child's response to the film *The Tap Dance Kid*: "The dad should have let his son go and audition. He was being very mean." Students also predicted, hypothesized, or conjectured at this level, as this child does in response to *The Great Gilly Hopkins*:

> I figure there must have been a lot of love in that house, especially when Gilly didn't want to even think about leaving—Gilly, who had learned, well, thought, that no

one could ever love her, and thought that she should never get attached to a foster home. I loved the book.

At this level, students also questioned or expressed wonder at story events. For example, in response to the film *Granny Lives in Galway,* one child writes: "One thing I wonder about is why did he want those children if he hated them?"

At the next level, responders began to leave the world of the story behind and demonstrated understandings of story events through analogy to themselves or the world. They began to open the confines of the text by placing themselves in situations from the text or by relating the characters or understandings of specific events to the real world. The literary world becomes an actual experience from which the reader gains understanding. One child does this in response to *Very Good Friends* as she writes: "It made you think about what you would do if someone very close to you died."

At the highest level, responders reached a generalized belief or understanding about life which is not tied to specific story events. The personal meaning becomes more global and applicable to the world in general rather than demonstrating understanding only in terms of specific situations as found in the text. In these types of responses, students reached generalizations, projected possible worlds, or stated a moral or a lesson.

Adrienne reached this level in her response to *Where the Red Fern Grows* cited earlier. She clearly moves beyond the words on the page and the world of the text as she imagines "the perfect place to grow up," a place where "time just stood still." Another child imagines a better world in his response to the film *The Case of the Elevator Duck:* "If more people were like the boy in this movie, the world would be better. It was kind of him to do what he did for the duck." Another comes to the conclusion that "children have rights too" in her response to *The Tap Dance Kid.* And others came to generalizations as they mused about things they themselves had experienced, as this child does in response to *The Great Gilly Hopkins:* "I wonder if this is what it is like to be a foster child. If so it is not the easiest thing in the world."

CHARACTERISTICS OF STUDENTS' RESPONSES: STANCE AND PERSONAL UNDERSTANDING

When viewed from a reader-response perspective and analyzed according to stance and personal understanding, these fifth-grade students' responses revealed several tendencies. First, there were differences between texts for both stance and personal understanding. Of the nine books and films, students responded aesthetically most often to *Summer of the Swans,* and efferently most often to *Phillip Hall Likes Me, I Reckon Maybe.* In terms of personal understanding, students were most likely to go beyond interpretation of story events and apply them to life in responses to *Summer of the Swans, The Fur Coat Club,* and *The Tap Dance Kid.* They were least likely to do this in response to *Phillip Hall Likes Me, I Reckon Maybe.* Second, the majority of these students' responses to both books and films were written from an aesthetic stance. In terms of personal understanding, the majority of responses went beyond the literal level of interpretation, and on the average more than one-fourth of the responses went beyond understandings tied to the world of the text and in some way were connected to life. Third, and perhaps most importantly, the aesthetic stance was most associated with the highest level of personal understanding.

TEACHING AESTHETICALLY WITH LITERATURE

When Nancy Cothern made the choice of using literature and writing as both a means and an end to language learning and instruction in her classroom, she gained control of her classroom. And in making this choice, she was able to offer greater choices to her students. The responses of Adrienne and Geneva and the other students in this classroom tell us several things about what happens when this occurs. When students are encouraged to read, view, dream, and think freely during transactions with literary works, they can and will respond aesthetically by focusing on the lived-through experience of reading and viewing events. And in so doing, they are empowered. They are empowered to the point where even in fifth grade, they are able to take interpretation beyond the words on the page or the one world created by the author. They are able to break through the boundaries of the text and make the literary experience their own. As they do, they create new worlds of meaning for themselves.

Teachers like Nancy have many other choices to make as they gain control through teaching aesthetically and supporting students in their efforts to respond aesthetically. One is to open classrooms to many forms of literariness. The use of film in this study afforded the same opportunities for higher levels of interpretation and personal understanding as books. Furthermore, the intertextual connections students made between stories in many different forms strengthened the aesthetic response and, consequently, understanding. Another choice to be made is to let students make choices about what they read and view. The between-text differences in terms of stance and understanding in this study suggest that not all students will respond efferently or aesthetically to the same book. And while some, like *Summer of the Swans,* seemed to provide more opportunity for an aesthetic transaction for many students, others responded aesthetically to other books and films. This implies that teachers question any kind of literary canon that might limit students' choices of text. To do so may limit their opportunities to read and respond aesthetically.

Students should be able to make choices about how they will provide for and organize their evocation of a text. Initially, students should be allowed the time and freedom to respond openly—to say or write anything they want about a text. When children in this class were allowed to do so, the majority of their responses were aesthetic, focusing on the lived-through experience of the work. The children's responses also give clues on ways to further support the aesthetic response. Students could be guided to picture and create images in their minds as they read, to relate intertextual and autobiographical associations and feelings, and to hypothesize, extend, and retrospect with regard to the literary evocation. And it is on these aesthetic responses that further inquiry or study of a text may be built.

Rosenblatt has suggested that the aesthetic stance is the most appropriate for literature (1982). She has also hypothesized that it is also the most neglected in schools, and recent studies confirm this (Cox and Zarrillo, 1990; Sacks, 1986). Teachers making choices about materials and methods in literature-based whole language classrooms gain control when they teach aesthetically by giving choices. And giving children the choice to focus on the lived-through experience of the work gives them control over their own ability to construct meaning while reading, viewing, and thinking aesthetically.

REFERENCES

Bruner, J. *Actual Minds, Possible Worlds.* Cambridge, Massachusetts: Harvard University Press, 1986.

Byars, B. *Summer of the Swans.* New York: Viking, 1970.

The Case of the Elevator Duck. Coronet/MTI/Learning Corporation of America.

Cox, C., and Many, J. E. "Reader stance towards a literary work: Applying the transactional theory to children's responses." Paper presented at the Annual Meeting of the American Educational Research Association, San Francisco, California, March 1989.

Cox, C., and Zarrillo, J. "Teaching With Literature in the Elementary Shool: A Qualitative Study Applying the Transactional Theory." Paper presented at the Annual Meeting of the American Educational Research Association, Boston, Massachusetts, April 1990.

The Fur Coat Club. Coronet/MTI/Learning Corporation of America.

Granny Lives in Galway. Coronet/MTI/Learning Corporation of America.

Greene, B. *Phillip Hall Likes Me, I Reckon Maybe.* New York: Dial, 1974.

Paterson, K. *The Great Gilly Hopkins.* New York: Harper & Row, 1978.

Rawls, W. *Where the Red Fern Grows.* New York: Doubleday, 1961.

Ricoeur, P. *Interpretation Theory: Discourse and the Surplus of Meaning.* Fort Worth: Texas Christian University Press, 1976.

Rosenblatt, L M. *The Reader, the Text, the Poem: The Transactional Theory of the Literary Work.* Carbondale, Illinois: Southern Illinois University Press, 1978.

Rosenblatt, L. M. "The Literary Transaction: Evocation and Response." *Theory Into Practice,* 21, 168-277, 1982.

Rosenblatt, L. M. "The Transactional Theory of the Literary Work." In C. R. Cooper (Ed.), *Researching Response to Literature and the Teaching of Literature* (pp. 33-53). Norwood, New Jersey: Ablex, 1985.

Rosenblatt, L. M. "The Aesthetic Transaction." *Journal of Aesthetic Education,* 20, 122-128, 1986.

Sacks, L. F. "Efferent and Aesthetic Modes in the Teaching of Poetry as Related to Teachers' Construal of Poetry." *Dissertation Abstracts International,* 48, 325A, 1986.

The Tap Dance Kid. Coronet/MTI/Learning Corporation of America.

Very Good Friends. Coronet/MTI/Learning Corporation of America.

Carole Cox is a faculty member at California State University, Long Beach.

BETTY BOSMA

Informational Books Provide Diversity in the Whole Language Classroom

I entered a kindergarten classroom in Grand Rapids, Michigan, and found a group of children gathered around the can of earthworms they had dug up earlier that day.

"How can we keep them alive?" they asked the teacher. Survival demands answers.

"Let's find out," answered Mrs. V., turning to a special bookcase filled with profusely illustrated informational books. Together they paged through *Our Earthworms* by Herbert Wong and Matthew Vessel, and the teacher read from the page the children thought had the answer. Later teacher and children followed Wong's directions closely and made a worm farm. When children visited the science table, they matched their farm with the pictures of the farm in the book.

"Children learn best when they are actively sharing the world," Mrs. V. reported to me, "but we also learn from what other people have discovered about the world. I want them to see that grown-ups need to learn from books just as children do."

A primary classroom at Bank Street School in New York City visited their neighborhood postal station and returned to school to build their own post office and sell stamps. The teacher read them several informational books in preparation for organizing and selling. Their two favorite books, which they pored over whenever they had time, were Mildred DePree's *A Child's World of Stamps* and a government document, *The Postal Service Guide to U.S. Stamps.* Although written for adults, the government document was interesting and informative, with pictures of commemorative stamps. A new document is published each year and available at local post offices.

In Upper Arlington, Ohio, a group of third- and fourth-graders was busy putting up displays of their work from a study of shapes and patterns. The intricate designs and long, explanatory paragraphs led me to ask the teacher again if this was really a third-and-fourth-grade classroom. I asked a boy how they had learned all that.

He replied:

> Well, in math, the teacher started asking us questions like "What's an angle?" "What's a dodecahedron?" "What's a parallelogram?" We didn't have any idea what anything was. Then she asked us what we might discover about these things, and we just started branching out.

Children explained to me how they began by making lists of shapes with the whole group, and then choosing the particular shape they wanted to study. I discovered that two had investigated the polyhedron and went on to study the history of geometry. The children who chose the hexagon included nature and honeybees in their study. A pupil told me how his group began their pyramid study:

> I thought you could just call them pyramids, but I found out that they can have a hexagonal or octagonal base. And then we went to Egypt in our books, and now we've got all these.

He proudly showed me the various paper pyramids they had constructed. Among the informational books they used were *Pyramid* by David Macauley, *Behind the Sealed Door,* by I. and L. Swinburne, and *Mummies Made in Egypt* by Aliki.

Denise Bartelo, a fifth-grade teacher in San Antonio, Texas, sent out an SOS call to her class to save the environment.

"Why does the earth have a Band-Aid on it?" asked Edwardo, as he looked at the bulletin board.

More questions followed, and Mrs. Bartelo introduced the book *S.O.S. Save Our Earth* by George Masini. The children answered their own questions by learning about technology, pollution, and food chains. They engaged in individual anecdotal observations, patterned after the model reports in *Understanding Ecology* by Elizabeth Billington, a book now out of print but possibly in your school library. An ecology checklist found in Betty Miles's *Save the Earth* helped them monitor their use of such resources as water and electricity. These particular books were written in the 1970s. In the early 1980s few ecology books were published, but now many authentic and interesting books address specific ecological concerns.

Jeanine Kemp of East Grand Rapids, Michigan, found many books on whales to tap second-graders' interest before launching an oceanography study. They sang along with Raffi and added original verses to "Baby Beluga." They read whale poems such as "Whale" from *The Limerick Book* by Miriam Troop. After hearing *Humphrey the Wrong Way Whale,* the children brainstormed the questions they had about whales. Seymour Simon's *Whales* offered exquisite photographs and simple text for them to study. The comparisons Simon made between whale size and familiar objects in the child's environment helped them understand these giant animals. Learning about whales by means of both fiction and nonfiction books led the children to create their own personal whales and write stories based on facts about that particular species.

What do these exciting classrooms throughout the country have in common? Each has a teacher who guides, directs, and encourages children to ask questions and look for their own answers in authentic, carefully illustrated, and clearly written informational books. These teachers replaced rigid time schedules with large blocks of time, knowing that children are learning reading, writing, math, science, and social studies concurrently.

In addition, these classrooms have current, well-written informational books. The informational books of the 1980s contrast with older books in school libraries because of their diversity of content and style. Instead of speaking in an omniscient, rational, distant manner, the narrators choose to be exuberant, humorous, personal, questioning, or probing. Laurence Pringle writes in *The Voice of the Narrator in Children's Literature:* "I tend to challenge authority and accepted truths. This has influenced my choice of subjects, as I have questioned popular but incorrect notions about forest fires, dinosaurs, vampire bats, wolves, coyotes, and killer bees. Part of my goal is to show that the process of science aims for a better understanding of the world. As long as we keep asking questions, that understanding can change" (p. 378). Pringle's look at ecology in *Throwing Things Away: From Middens to Resource Recovery* offers complex interconnections, including archaeology, dumps and landfills, and wildlife scavengers.

Elementary teachers can take an active role in encouraging media-resource directors to update the informational book holdings in their schools. Book selection aid can be found in many current journals. The following professional journals include nonfiction book reviews: *The Arithmetic Teacher, Science and Children, Social Education, The Reading Teacher, Language Arts,* and *The Elementary School Journal.* Each year the American Library Association collaborates with the National Council for the Social Studies to publish *Notable Children's Trade Books in the Field of the Social Studies* and with the National Science Teachers Association to select and publish *Outstanding Science Trade Books for Children.* These lists include both nonfiction and related fiction. Both of these are available from the Children's Book Council for the price of a stamped self-addressed envelope.

To promote and recognize excellence in the writing of nonfiction for children, the National Council of Teachers of English has authorized a book award, The Orbis Pictus Award for Outstanding Nonfiction for Children. The first award will be given in 1990 for the best nonfiction book written in 1989. The literary criteria for selection include accuracy, organization, design, and style of writing. In addition, the award book should be useful in classroom teaching. It should encourage thinking and more reading, model exemplary expository writing and research skills, share interesting and timely subject matter, and appeal to a wide range of ages.

Informational books play an important role in the whole language classroom, where teachers are committed to encourage and extend the natural curiosity of their students. A teacher who makes the switch from depending on textbooks for information gathering to quality trade books for information seeking will find a new joy in learning that will be actively shared with their students.

REFERENCES

Aliki (Aliki Brandenberg). *Mummies Made in Egypt*. New York: Crowell, 1979.

Billington, Elizabeth. *Understanding Ecology*. (Out of print.) A good general reference that may be in your school library.

DePree, Mildred. *A Child's World of Stamps: Stories, Poems, Fun and Facts From Many Lands*. Parents Magazine Press, in cooperation with the U.S. Committee for UNICEF, 1973.

Goldner, K. and Vogel, C. *Humphrey the Wrong Way Whale*. New York: Dillon, 1987.

Macaulay, David. *Pyramid*. Boston: Houghton Mifflin, 1975.

Masini, George. *S.O.S. Save Our Earth*. New York: Wm. Collins, 1972.

Miles, Betty. *Save the Earth. An Ecology Handbook for Kids*. New York: Knopf, 1974.

Otten, C. and Schmidt, G. (Eds.) *The Voice of the Narrator in Children's Literature*. New York: Greenwood Press, 1989.

Pringle, Laurence. *Throwing Things Away: From Middens to Resource Recovery*. New York: Crowell, 1986.

Raffi. "Baby Beluga." *Songs for Children and the Young at Heart*, 4th album. A & M Records, 1980.

Simon, Seymour. *Whales*. New York: Crowell, 1989.

Swinburne, I. and Swinburne, L. *Behind the Sealed Door: Tomb and Treasures of Tutankhamun*. New York: Sniffen Court, 1978.

Troop, M. *The Limerick Book*. New York: Grosset and Dunlap, 1984.

United States Postal Service Mint Set of Commemorative Stamps. Government document published annually.

Wong, H. and Vessel, M. *Our Earthworms*. New York: Addison-Wesley, 1977.

Professional Journals With Book Reviews

The Arithmetic Teacher. National Council of Teachers of Mathematics. 1906 Association Drive. Reston, VA 22091.

The Reading Teacher. International Reading Association. 800 Barksdale Road, P.O. Box 8139, Newark, DE 19714-8139.

Language Arts. National Council of Teachers of English. 1111 Kenyon Road, Urbana, IL 61801.

Elementary School Journal. The University of Chicago Press. 5801 S. Ellis, Chicago, IL 61637.

Social Education. National Council for Social Studies, 35011 Newark Street, NW, Washington, DC 20016

Science and Children. National Science Teachers Association. P.O. Box 3710 Dept. 5013. Jefferson City, MO 65120-9957.

For lists of Outstanding Science and Social Studies books, write to the Children's Book Council, 67 Irving Place, P.O. Box 706, New York, NY 10276-0706.

Betty Bosma is a faculty member at Calvin College, in Grand Rapids Michigan.

NANCY HOWELL, LYNN POTT,
AND MARION SIEFERT

Readers of Literature, Makers of Literature

Following are three perspectives on teacher empowerment, which discuss three components of our program at Bellerive Elementary School in St. Louis County, Missouri. Our school has been recognized by the American School Board and *Executive Editor* as having one of the "100 best curriculum ideas in the nation." It is also an NCTE Center for Excellence site school for our language-arts program. We are currently a finalist for the IRA Exemplary Reading Program award.

WRITING WORKSHOP
LYNN POTT

"Carpe diem: Seize the day" were words spoken by Robin Williams in the movie *Dead Poets Society.* Are these words also tucked away in the unspoken vocabulary of empowered whole language teachers? We think they are.

Robin Williams portrayed a teacher who wanted students to love language. He wanted them to look at the world in a different way and think for themselves. Robin Williams went against tradition as he taught the love of words through enthusiastic reading and student involvement, not through the predetermined strategies that were listed in a book. He was a risk taker.

Whole language teachers are also risk takers. They are not relying on the basals for their next lesson. Instead, they are researching their students to discover what the next lesson will be. A risk-taking teacher is an empowered teacher.

Teacher empowerment is not possible unless the principal believes in the current research. It is fortunate for me that my principal is a strong reader of current research and a risk taker himself. Otherwise I would still be using the basal for my teaching strategies.

When teachers feel empowered, they begin to feel like professionals. They make the decisions about what to teach their students, not a textbook. They learn to evaluate and listen. I learned as my students learned.

I was fortunate to be able to attend Donald Graves's workshop and the summer classes given by Mary Ellen Giacobbe, Nancy Atwell, and Lucy Calkins. They taught me how to learn from my students. When I began utilizing the writing workshop, I was skeptical and unsure of myself. Mary Ellen became my mentor. Being the gracious and dedicated educator that she is, she would explain different ways to solve the problems. She is indeed an asset to education.

Also, the teachers in my building allow me to teach the writing workshop at the other grade levels. They let me work with their classes. Being a fifth-grade teacher, I need to understand the different stages before they reach me. I have learned so much.

The writing workshop forces teachers and students to grow. It definitely teaches students to write. They are forced to evaluate their writing and the writing of others. They also learn to look at other authors with the critical eye of a writer. The students begin to analyze, synthesize, and evaluate literature, because they are makers of literature.

The writing workshop includes a minilesson, a status of the class, conferencing, and author sharing. Mary Ellen Giacobbe uses three key words to describe this researched strategy: time, ownership, and response

Time refers to the importance of having our students write at a specific time each day, for four to five days each week. They need this structure to grow as writers. Students learn to rehearse ideas, draft, revise, conference, and publish.

Ownership refers to the students' writing about what they are experts on. How can we expect our students to be good writers if we give them topics that they don't care about or don't know about? When they care about their story, they will do their best to make it perfect. They want their stories to be understood. They are proud. When they are proud, they will also try hard to make a final copy mechanically correct. They learn in the context of their own writing. *Response* refers to the conferencing that takes place between the students and the teachers or the students and the students. I learned that it is extremely important for writers to get feedback from others. They need to hear their pieces read aloud. This helps them catch their own errors.

Teacher empowerment is part of each aspect of the writing workshop structure, which includes a minilesson, a status of the class (developed by Nancy Atwell), conferencing, and author sharing. The five-to-ten-minute minilesson introduces strategies for the students to utilize. The status of the class helps the teacher know what the students will be doing and makes the students responsible. Conferencing lets the students know the teacher cares, because the teacher works individually with them. Students learn to think as they are asked questions about their writing. Finally, the author sharing helps the writers get feedback and recognition for good writing as the students help their classmate improve the piece of writing.

Writing workshop also empowers students. They are making decisions as they write. They, not the teacher, decide when they have a good piece to publish. Decisions about genre, topic, form, leads, endings, etc. are also made by the student. They learn to think for themselves. Isn't this what education is all about?

Before I began the writing workshop, I taught writing, but I realize that my students didn't really grow as writers. I was furnishing the topic and the motivations. I made suggestions on how to improve their writing, then they copied their stories over and turned them in. I taught as I was taught.

Part of me still does this, but in an empowered way. In our district we are required to teach the basal skills and test the students on their proficiency. As a result, the students are pretested to determine which skills they need to work on and which ones need only a review. This is how more time is found to teach the writing workshop. We teach three separate levels of reading, but I rotate the groups. Teaching skills is not teaching reading, but we believe that teaching them strategies will not inhibit their growth either. It is necessary to work within a system. Part of empowerment relates to making a program work, even if parameters are needed. Our total program in fifth grade includes the writing workshop, reading workshop, vocabulary workshop, literature sets, and thematic integration. Each component has been added as we teacher researchers have been given empowerment to grow. As a result, I have grown and I continue to learn. In *Dead Poets Society*, they never referred to Robin Williams as an empowered teacher or a whole language teacher. I think he was.

Whole language teachers (i.e., empowered teachers) do "seize the day and look at the world in a different way." Isn't that what education is all about?

LITERATURE SETS
NANCY HOWELL

It is a universal theory that, in order for goals to be useful, they must be linked to a mission. The same theory applied to the classroom empowerment of teacher and students wanting to change strategies and procedures of the reading and language-arts curriculum in our school. In order to initiate change, students and teachers were motivated by a mission. They knew this mission often appears out of a need for change. Powerful instructional goals were used to guide the program toward our school mission. It was simply . . . . to have a schoolful of students who love to read and write.

First of all, a good gauge that something was wrong with the reading program was determined by student comments such as "We just want to read the stories and skip all that other stuff." Our teachers wanted to see them doing just that. Teaching skills isolated from meaning was a tiring task for both teachers and students. Skill instruction was not directed toward immediate application. Results could not be seen; therefore, something needed to be changed. The teachers saw it. The students saw it

Once our teachers were aware of this need for change, it was important that the ability to initiate this change was available. Many class-rooms have teachers who are on "a lonely island" in their building when it comes to implementing change in their curriculum. They are either the only teacher thinking about such changes, or they have attempted to change behind "closed doors." Valuable, wholesome changes, directed toward the good of students, are best when made available through the administration. Good teachers will begin to ask these questions, as we did: Why is it that students do not use the library or enjoy reading in their leisure time? Why do our students seldom have informal dialogue about books they've read, as they do about movies they've seen?

Next, an initiation of events, which includes the evaluation of condi-tions in the current reading program, began. This included staff develop-ment programs designed to assist the principal and teachers in implement-ing their philosophy and mission with the curriculum.

This is the point where student empowerment was the greatest. It only took a spark of an idea, a few methods for implementation, and the students' input. We believe that instructors are at their best when they treat the students as equals. We asked them why they didn't enjoy reading. What was the problem? What could be changed? How could we arrange our day to focus around good books? What will work best for us? What do you want to see happen? How can we accomplish this? When will we get time? Where will we put the materials? All students participated. The input from the least-suspected student was a delight for the teacher. Excellent teaching occurs when the students consider and trust the teacher as one of them. Once students are empowered, they must continue to be empowered. Their help can't be enlisted and dropped. It must be an ongoing system of teacher-student interaction and trust.

Once we knew that writing workshop and literature sets were consistent with our mission, work commenced. We knew literature should be fun, enjoyable, exciting, stimulating, and much more. So what kind of literature-based program did we want? Response groups, reading multiple copies of books and journal logs, provided opportunities for thinking, speaking, listening, reading, and writing. The structure of our literature-sets groups is students choosing the books to read and writing a response to share in the group, with teachers as facilitators. We wanted this to become not a comprehension drill about facts but a response about how the student thinks and feels toward the selection. That program, coupled with teachers who knew all kinds of literature from all sorts of places, and who cared about sharing literature with students, was a sure-fire hit. If the teacher cares and is enthusiastic about books, students will pick up on the atmosphere and be hooked on books forever. Book lovers are made, not born.

The next step of teacher-student empowerment took time, organization, and effort. The teachers prepared days, even weeks, in advance for a change from the traditional language-arts program. First, they coordinated their plans with the administrator. They developed minilessons, chose multiple copies of books, enlisted parent support, decided how to handle difficult students, and made a multitude of decisions. They remembered that students are willing helpers and brilliant idea banks. Not only was empowering students important, but empowering co-workers through teamwork reaped tremendous results. All of these tactics helped to expedite change toward the implementation of a whole language program in our school.

Each phase of change took time and effort on the part of both administrators and teachers. Making the change a routine part of the day and refining weak areas were paramount in the success of our program. Valuable, wholesome changes in the curriculum must have a systematic method of evaluation for ways to improve it. Are the students enjoying their reading through literature sets? Are they using the services of the librarian more now than before? Do they know books and authors? Our whole language program is oriented around results and what is good for kids. There is a guarantee of this when a strong literature-based reading program is part of the school curriculum.

THE INTEGRATED CURRICULUM
MARION SIEFERT

Integration extends the philosophy of whole language by centering on learning in three areas. These are (1) learning as a lifetime pursuit, (2) learning that focuses on a holistic approach rather than the isolation of disciplines, and (3) process learning, which integrates reading and writing across the curriculum. Through whole language, teachers assume the responsibility of teaching as well as making learning an enjoyable pursuit while empowering the student. Beginning with the traditional curriculum, teachers incorporate active learning with units that capitalize on the wholeness of the curriculum. As teachers begin integration, they start with several non-negotiable tools—district-level scope and sequence charts, curriculum guides, basal texts, school-board policies, etc. Within the traditional framework they can brainstorm to incorporate units of study built around integrated topics. As teachers integrate, the focal point should be the interrelated application of skills and strategies to all disciplines.

I understand that this may appear insurmountable. However, with a commitment of ample time and advanced planning of a yearlong framework, teacher and student empowerment will become a natural part of the curriculum. When teachers first begin this process of integration, it is helpful to look at each of the various disciplines for similar topics. Teachers on each grade level can connect the units and chapters of each discipline into various topics. The next step will be refinement, as teachers match these units with the required district curriculum, scope and sequence, and testing programs. Within these units, teachers can select literature to incorporate, thus exposing students to various genres and authors' styles. At this time, student empowerment becomes a factor as they are given a choice of the incorporated literature. The literatures along with the factual material gleaned from the curriculum can be used as a basis for students' writing as they become an expert on the topics they have chosen to study. Using the broad curriculum topics, teachers can develop a framework for extended activities/projects, thus allowing student interests and abilities to determine the method of further research and the mode by which this knowledge will be shared with others.

The next step in developing an integrated curriculum is one in which the teacher and student, along with the wider community, all become learners as the new curriculum is implemented. Empowerment comes by way of introduction to new philosophies and strategies through research and staff development. Thus a nurturing environment is developed in which teachers are encouraged to "risk to learn." As new strategies are developed, mentoring and coaching become a vital part of the community of learners in which the standard role of teacher is transformed. As teachers implement new strategies, they must incorporate these into their own style of teaching. As whole language implies, there is no set method of teaching, only continual learning and refining. Teachers working with the new curriculum develop their own personal strategies as they learn with their students.

As teachers develop strategies, decisions are made about learning, whereby the individual needs and interests of each student are taken into account. An empowered curriculum needs to have the structure to meet state and district requirements while allowing for continual modification to meet the individual needs of all students. These can be provided through a variety of student groupings. Whole classroom instruction can provide students with a common background of knowledge and a foundation for individual interests. Small-group instruction is twofold; interest groups for the discussion of literature read and project development or instructional groups for specific students in need of further guidance or explanation. Students can be provided with individual instruction and modification of the curriculum, whether it be for acceleration or remediation. An integrated curriculum allows all students to become a part of the learning process by allowing them to contribute their expertise as they learn holistically.

Nancy Howell, Lynn Pott, and Marion Siefert are classroom teachers at Bellerive Elementary School in St. Louis County, Missouri.

GORDON ANDERSON

Teacher Transition From a Skills to a Whole Language Classroom

Whole language is a grass-roots movement that has been sweeping the country over the past several years. It is a philosophy of literacy learning whose theory and model of learning emerged from socio-psycholinguistic research and practice. Whole language views children as capable learners who bring language strengths and experiences to learning tasks and learn language easily when it is meaningful, contextual, functional, and natural. When put into practice, this view engages learners in holistic use of all the language processes—speaking, listening, reading, and writing—for real, communicative purposes. Language cues (graphophonemic, syntactic, and semantic) and learning strategies (sampling, predicting, confirming, correcting, and integrating) are kept intact and imbedded in the communicative act.

Many administrators and parents have observed the positive impact whole language has upon learners and literacy and have become interested in and enthusiastic about whole language. Along with teachers, they have increasingly observed that students don't learn and use literacy effectively—nor do they like to read—when language is fragmented through a prescribed skills curriculum that dictates materials and tests.

Teachers' theoretical understanding about the language-learning process—what they believe about how children learn and use language—influences all their interactions with students.

SKILLS TEACHERS' BELIEFS AND PRACTICES

A skills view believes that language is learned by practicing each skill in isolation and leads teachers to lean on a prescribed basal reader's materials. Teachers assume the validity of the scope and sequence of skills mandated by the publisher whose spelling, reading, and grammar workbooks and textbooks consume productive time. The practice of skills is generally separated from authentic uses of reading and writing, and it is assumed that learners will transfer isolated practice and drill to real-life tasks. Real literature becomes a time filler, and only limited time is provided for holistic and sustained use of language.

Evaluation, too, becomes separated into skills areas apart from authentic use. A management system frequently accompanies the basal and provides tests at the end of each level to determine the rate at which each child progresses—or fails to progress—in reading. Criteria-achievement levels require fixed and inflexible grouping of children according to perceived ability. Under direct prescription by the basal, the teacher must control learning.

WHOLE LANGUAGE TEACHERS' BELIEFS AND PRACTICES

In contrast, the whole language teacher believes that language is best learned from whole to part in meaningful, functional, and social contexts. The personal experiences and interests of students become the focal point of activity as learners are encouraged to take risks while learning to read and write. Students are trusted to make choices, retain ownership of reading and writing efforts, and participate in collaborative learning with peers and teachers as they become independent learners.

Classroom practice integrates language processes as children use literacy authentically and collaboratively. Conferences with teachers and peers provide a supportive environment in which teachers evaluate reading and writing in processing—often in concert with learners' self-evaluations.

Grouping in this setting becomes flexible as children engage in writing workshops and read self-selected books. In order to learn from and with each other, students move freely to meet with peers of select materials.

FACTORS INHIBITING CHANGE

The transition to a different, less teacher-controlled approach is often difficult. The will to change may be thwarted by administrative mandates to follow a prescribed curriculum and use district-purchased materials. An administrative yen to maintain the status quo may discourage teachers from straying from the established course.

With a long history of text and system dependency, teachers, as a group, have not had a voice in building curriculum and may be inexperienced in making terms of selecting and using materials and methods. They may have lost their own sense of professional competence and fear the risk involved in the move to whole language.

Another inhibiting factor is the requirement that teachers give mandated basal, competency, or standardized tests that stem directly from the skills-oriented approach. Many teachers feel a sense of guilt; they fear that if they teach more holistically, they will leave out something vitally needed for these tests.

Despite these inhibiting factors, thousands of teachers are taking the risks and making the changes.

WHY TEACHERS CHANGE

Fighting against administrative mandates, lack of voice, accountability tests, and guilt feelings, many teachers have persevered in doing what they believe is best for kids.

Some make the transition out of frustration with the prescribed skills curriculum, whose total control seems antithetical to language learning. Others have observed the devastating effects basal programs have on reading and writing development and attitude.

Increasingly, teachers are observing firsthand the richness and pleasure inherent in the learning environment of whole language classrooms where learners make choices, share with peers, and read and write for personally meaningful purposes. Observation of colleagues helps interested teachers become apprentices who learn how to read aloud, encourage learner choice of books, establish writing workshops, and engage learners in sustained reading and writing.

Many teachers turn to supportive colleagues in TAWL groups where they share ideas, successes, and frustrations in their own community of learners. That support is vital during this transition.

A crucial element in making the transition is the process of becoming familiar with whole language through reading professional literature and understanding the research that undergirds whole language practice. The writings of Frank Smith, Ken and Yetta Goodman, Dorothy Watson, Donald Graves, Lucy Calkins, Nancie Atwell, and others provide both support for the beginner and sustenance for the veteran. The increasing variety of conferences and workshops offered through universities and national and regional organizations provides additional resources where theory and practice can be developed and explored.

MAKING THE CHANGE

There is no absolute blueprint for teachers to follow during this transition. Each teacher is unique in terms of personality, situation, experience, and style, but a belief in the need for the transition and the will to reach out to supportive resources and colleagues make it possible. A crucial factor is the need to articulate to others (parents, administrators, and skills-oriented colleagues) the rationale for whole language activity and the research findings that support it.

The transition from skills to whole language is often gradual. Teachers may slowly phase out basal programs as the dominant materials by introducing literature study part of the time, scheduling writing workshop on some days, and increasing the time devoted to silent reading.

Anderson (1984) has identified and described four incremental stages teachers may go through as they change over time from a skills to a whole language classroom. The model includes four overlapping stages, each of which describes how teachers change their use of interrelated components of classroom organization and management. Individual teachers will vary the components that are changed and the rate of change from a traditional skills to a whole language classroom. The chart on the next page outlines briefly the four interrelated stages, components, and common characteristics of each stage and component.

	STAGE 1: TRADITIONAL SKILLS CLASSROOM	STAGE 2: MODIFIED TRADITONAL CLASSROOM	STAGE 3: TRADITIONAL WHOLE LANGUAGE CLASSROOM	STAGE 4: WHOLE LANGUAGE CLASSROOM
PERSONNEL	One Teacher	One Teacher One Aide	One Teacher Two Aides	One Teacher Three Aides
TIME	Separate time periods for reading, spelling, math content	Language Arts block in morning, Content block in afternoon	Language Arts block in the morning, Content block in afternoon	Language Arts and content time integrates all day
SPACE	Desks chairs in rows Teacher desk in front Inflexible, static use of space	Desks, chairs clustered together One or two learning centers	Tables, desks, chairs arranged for groups Two or three learning centers Children choose space	Flexible use of space Several learning Language and content Teacher desk at side of classroom
METHODS, MATERIALS, LEARNING EXPERIENCES	Basal reader Workbooks Skill ditto sheets Letter-sound games Word games Some SSR Textbooks (social studies, sciences)	Basal reader Some wprkbooks More SSR More SSW Reading center Writing center	Literature Basal reader (incidental) No workbooks or worksheets SSR-literature SSW Reading, writing center activities	Teacher read-aloud Assisted reading Language experience SSR SSW Reading and writing samples Arts Music Thematic units
EVALUATION	Basal reader tests Isolated skills tests Workbooks Worksheets Teacher-made tests Textbook tests	Basal reader tests Workbooks tests Teacher observations Reading and writing samples	RMI Some basal reader tests Teacher observation during SSR SSW Learning center activities Cloze test IRI	Teacher observation Reading and writing samples RMW Cloze tests Student self-evaluation
GROUPING	Achievement groups Independent seat work Workbooks Worksheets Skill ditto sheets	Some achievement groups Independent and group reading Independent and group writing	Independent reading and writing Art projects Sharing session Learning centers	Individual and group activities SSR SSW Thematic units Research units Strategy groups Interest groups Sharing sessions

COPING WITH THE TRANSITION

Change is neither easy nor painless—personally or professionally. In the past curricular change has been mandated from above; rarely has innovation been developed at the grass-roots level, where teachers work and learn every day. While teachers have served on basal-reader and textbook-adoption committees, this resulted in minimum ownership—the option not to adopt the text hasn't existed. The move to whole language necessitates involvement with administrators, boards of education, and parents; each must have ownership and input. When districts establish genuine and general literacy goals and building principals are knowledgeable and supportive enough to encourage teacher autonomy, they can all work in concert to put in place classroom practice that develops literacy in all students.

The transition to whole language reduces rather than adds to educational burdens for all concerned. Change should be gradual and voluntary as all participants share new and exciting experiences.

REFERENCE

Anderson, Gordon S. *A Whole Language Approach to Reading*. Lanham, Maryland: University Press of America, 1984.

Gordon Anderson is a faculty member at the University of Dayton, in Dayton Ohio.

FRANCINE S. BALLAN AND STEVEN TRIBUS

"Scholars dispute, and the case is still before the courts" (Horace)

THE CONFLICT OVER ASSESSMENT

We encounter the frustrations that students feel as they take tests in *First Grade Takes A Test,* [1] by Miriam Cohen. The book that now needs to be written might be called *First-Grade Teachers Give A Test.* It is a fact of life for most schools but especially those in urban school districts that there are a host of legislative and societal demands for information about how well schools are carrying out their responsibilities to educate the young. Invariably, the single most popular instrument used for making such a determination is the standardized test, usually the standardized reading test.

The use of tests to measure student achievement causes major problems for teachers and schools that hope to implement an instructional program that reflects whole language philosophy and that places the responsibility for assessing students' progress where it belongs—on the classroom teacher. Such teachers, in districts where standardized tests are used as the indicator of the district's effectiveness, are faced with a dilemma. Most likely, the preparation that students need to be successful on these tests is antithetical to whole language instruction.

Allan Glatthorn (North Carolina State and East Carolina Universities) indicates that there is a "paradox inherent in the burgeoning teacher-professionalism movement and the proliferation of external controls on what must be taught in classrooms." Glatthorn points out that "there is a real tension that leaders in the field have to address."[2] Further, the focus of these external tests omits significant aspects of students' instruction such as how many books they have read, their attitudes toward reading, their assumption of responsibility for their learning and many other important aspects of a whole language classroom that defy assessment on standardized tests.

There is presently a call for more testing of more subjects, and the recent National Assessment of Educational Progress report[3] points to the need for stricter requirements (thus, by implication calling for more tests!). We need to raise questions as to how school districts can support their teachers' increasing demands to implement whole language in their classrooms. At the same time, they must meet economic and legislative demands to provide acceptably valid information on student performance. This article offers suggestions toward that end, while raising some critical issues that need to be addressed by both administrative and teaching staff as well as by the school boards and legislators who oversee these school personnel.

One need only observe schools at various times during the year to understand the problems generated by current standardized testing programs. Instead of having results influence instruction, the tests themselves drive instruction. Teachers and administrators who come together to plan in September often find themselves reviewing the tests and setting objectives that reflect the items they include. Happily, we have seen many schools that have found ways to develop curricula based on the needs of their students, where a whole language philosophy is embraced and where teacher judgment is valued. However, there are still too many schools where one encounters a feeling of frustration typified by remarks such as "I'd love to teach X, but I have to cover everything that will be on the test." It now seems possible that if the move toward a national curriculum and more testing continues, we may find ourselves with no place for teachers' judgment and no time to teach the things they feel are important. This current trend has allowed tests to have an influence beyond their stated purpose.

Approximately one month before "the test," the mood in the school changes. No longer do we see the exciting literary discussions and real writing that take place at other times; instead, it's time for test preparation. Whole instructional periods are planned for reviewing test procedures and taking practice tests. One is no longer shocked to see a daily plan that lists

"Multiple Choice: 10:00-11:00 a.m." on the chalkboard. In many classes, students who are asked what they are studying cancel all "extra" activities during this test-preparation month. This translates as no trips, no art, no music, and no reading that isn't directly related to the test. Reading for pleasure is put on the back burner until after the test. The inordinate amount of time spent on test preparation at those schools is at the expense of the valuable learning time that proponents of curriculum reform advocate.

In schools where the test fever has not struck, there is a healthy balance of adherence to the regular curriculum, while some time is set aside for learning about test practices. These schools recognize the need for students to be familiar with what is required on various standardized tests but continue to emphasize appropriate learning activities in classrooms.

The influence of standardized tests reaches far beyond the individual class. The publication of scores tends to pit one school against another as judgments about students, teachers, and administrators are often made on the basis of test results rather than on the general feeling in the schools, the student's attitudes towards learning, and an examination of their work. These areas, which define the accomplishments of whole language classes, are not considered newsworthy. As the emphasis on test results grows, so does the influence they generate. Several publishing companies are producing textbooks designed to help children score better, omitting areas that will probably not be tested. We have already seen workbooks designed to teach the items listed in *Cultural Literacy*.[4] Topics are given enough coverage so that a student can select the appropriate multiple-choice answer on the test, but nothing is discussed in depth.

The pressure to find a balance between appropriate teaching and appropriate assessment is one that we have been dealing with in New York City schools. We have been gratified to see that in schools where a whole language approach is encouraged, students are engaged in activities such as shared reading, literature-response groups, writing as a process, and thematic and cooperative learning. An issue that remains for these schools is the identification, development, and implementation of assessment instruments that reflect this type of instruction.

The support of the New York State Education Department and the Communication Arts Unit of the New York City Board of Education has enabled teachers to develop assessment instruments based on the activities in which their students are engaged. Teachers and administrators who were brought together under the CIMS-Communication Arts project network shared whole language strategies, defined instructional goals, explored literature, and designed curriculum. While they were pleased with the resultant changes they were making in their classrooms, most adhered to the type of testing they were familiar with: spelling, vocabulary, and comprehension tests on Fridays and social studies tests at the end of each unit. The need for developing alternative methods of assessment was clear. In response to this need, teachers and administrators were provided with opportunities to learn how to design assessment instruments. Most importantly, they also learned to recognize their instructional implications. What we observed in these schools was a shift to less time spent on tests and test preparation and more time spent on learning activities. As teachers understood the connections between learning and assessment they began to use the information gained from instruments to plan instruction. In addition, an analysis of these students' performance on standardized tests indicates that they scored significantly higher than their peers who had extensive test preparation. Meaningful learning activities had not hurt them one bit!

Given the dilemma that teachers and administrators face and the experiences that we have had in helping them cope with the problems that the development and implementation of alternate forms of assessment present, we suggest that there are several steps that districts and schools need to take if we are to make the process of assessment both useful and supportive of instruction. The common goal among these steps is to bring assessment practices in line with whole language teaching practices while recognizing the various needs that exist for tests in school districts.

First, state and local legislators need to reevaluate the reasons for their testing programs. Teacher and administrator groups, in concert with reading and English associations, must initiate campaigns to make legislators aware of the problems that have developed because of the harmful effects that tests have had on instruction. States need to identify and/or develop assessment policies and practices that support the instructional programs that they themselves support. Unfortunately, many states are advocating a whole language approach to teaching without a concomitant shift in their assessment programs. This redirection for assessment is particularly necessary because of the recent call for a national setting of curriculum and assessment standards. The November 1989 edition of the *ASCD Update* refers to the Gallup/Phi Delta Kappa poll released in August 1989 in which 70 percent of those polled "favored requiring public schools to conform to national achievement standards and goals." It is crucial, therefore, for educators to shape this movement so that it focuses on what's important in classrooms, not what's able to be measured.

Enlightened state governments and local boards of education should enlist teachers in helping to decide what assessments are to be required of schools. They should look for ways to use assessments as guideposts toward more effective instruction rather than as monitors of the acquisition of subskills. Further, we need to embark on an education program so that those who establish and implement assessment policies are taught new ways of looking at schools and classrooms, such as evaluating the role of the library in the schools and the number of books read by the students examining portfolios of writing that students consider their best work, identifying the various ways in which students respond to the literature they have read, and identifying the ways in which oral language instruction and activities permeate the school.

Second, if a school district moves toward alternative forms of testing while maintaining a standardized test, that test needs to be one where the preparation for success on it is through the kind of teaching practices that are in keeping with whole language philosophy. That is, we need to ensure that teachers are not made into educational schizophrenics who use one set of practices to teach and another set to prepare their students for taking tests.

Third, district personnel need to meet with teachers and administrators in order to set goals and objectives that reflect what's best for students, rather than what will be tested. Toward that end, an awareness campaign must be undertaken to help the general public understand what's important in evaluating schools instead of simply looking at a set of figures produced by standardized tests. Once this is done, the task of looking for ways to assess how well students are progressing will yield methods that respect the uniqueness of each child and the professionalism and creativeness of the teacher. With this shifted perspective, we will be better able to determine if their schools are making progress and ensure that students are acquiring concepts and skills and are engaging in educational experiences necessary to become successful, well-rounded members of society.

We are clearly at a crossroads between an emerging and expanding whole language approach to instruction and an antiquated and, in many cases, harmful approach to assessment. What do we really want to know about our schools and its students? What are the best ways to gain such insights? What role should teachers have in determining what is really important in our classrooms? How will we meet the legitimate needs of legislators and others to measure schools' effectiveness? How we handle this crisis and answer these questions will either continue to cause teachers and administrators to engage in practices that conflict with their own best judgment or speed along the day when what we do in classrooms becomes the centerpiece around which the rest of the educational establishment revolves. The whole language movement offers the best hope in a very long time to push these issues to center stage so that they might be resolved to the benefit of our students.

NOTES

1. Cohen, M. *First Grade Takes a Test.* New York: Dell, 1983.

2. *ASCD Update,* Vol. 31, No. 4, June 1989.

3. *National Assessment of Educational Progress,* 1/9/90.

4. Hirsch, Jr., E.D. *Cultural Literacy: What Every American Needs to Know.* Boston, Massachusetts: Houghton Mifflin, 1987.

Francine Ballan and Steven Tribus are educators with the New York City Public Schools.

Perspective From a TAWL Teacher

Change is possible! We can forsake the unyielding stone structures for the warmth and freedom of the garden trellis. Anderson's advice to listen to those at the forefront of research and experience is well founded. Where do we find them? Look in your classroom and those around you. All teachers are learners and researchers, as illustrated by the experiences shared here.

As we close our Day of Whole Language, turn with me to concluding perspectives from some who have been at the chalk face of research and experience from the beginning of this grass-roots movement. They have learned how to trust themselves and their learners and support those of us who are experiencing or want to experience the successes and excitement of whole language.

KENNETH S. GOODMAN

The Whole Language Curriculum
PLENARY SESSION III

What a wonderful day, and what a milestone in American education, North American education, and whole language in general. We'll talk about curriculum this afternoon and start with a riddle: Why is whole language whole language? Because it isn't part language. As teachers you know you sometimes hear yourself saying something that sounds pretty good, like comedians who tell themselves jokes they haven't heard before. In fact, teaching is probably the best way I know to learn something. You want to learn something, give yourself the task of teaching it. Now when I first heard myself say that riddle, I thought I was just making a pun. But I realized we developed a tradition, which got set in the concrete of report cards and tests and even the lesson-plan books that teachers use or are required to use, that broke language into parts rather than treating it as a whole. And the more I thought about it, the more I realized we had really developed a part-language curriculum.

THE PART-LANGUAGE CURRICULUM

Lately I've been asking the question "Why does spelling deserve its own place on the report card?" What's so important about spelling? The year before I got my doctorate, Yetta and I worked seventeen jobs and made a total of $5,000. One of her jobs was substitute teacher, which she could do as a mother of young children. She came home with a story of being in a teachers' lounge when a second-grade teacher came in, slammed down a book on a table, and said, "I'm not going to let those kids write another word until they learn how to spell."

Well, one of the things we have come to understand is that the importance of spelling is as a part of writing, and if you don't write there's no reason to spell. What Frank Smith and others have said about reading like a writer is, if you don't write you don't learn from reading about how spelling works. When you focus on the parts as ends in themselves, you lose any sense of their functional significance in authentic language.

The pain of my young life as a schoolboy was handwriting. Many of us can remember suffering through that. I still remember my humiliation with the push-pulls that I had to do and endless lines of spirals that got worse instead of better through meaningless practice. I moved a lot when I was in elementary school, and every time we moved I had to change the way I made my Rs and Ns.

Since then I have discovered something. You can't copyright a handwriting program unless it has substantial differences from all other handwriting programs. So the reason I had to keep changing was that they were using different handwriting texts. In the part-language curriculum, the textbook becomes the curriculum. There is no sense to the program except in the arbitrary choices made by the authors and editors.

Because we didn't have a sense of the significance of the whole or for that matter how to go about helping kids to develop language as a whole, we broke it into pieces, took it out of context, and made handwriting the torture I had to go through. And we made spelling torture for some kids too.

Ironically, sometimes kids get used to focusing on meaningless parts of language. It was a great surprise to me when I started teaching as a teacher in a self-contained eighth grade in Southern California and I did a little poll of my students that the favorite subject of the majority of my students was spelling and the least favorite was social studies. I was building around social studies, so that really hurt. Then I began to realize what they have learned to like about spelling was how isolated and finite it is. You've got so many words, you learn them or you don't learn them, and you're done. And often you get rewarded for what you knew before the lesson.

Social studies, on the other hand is open-ended. Social studies meant their having to take some responsibility for making some decisions, and that was harder. Now David Bloome calls what we have intentionally or unintentionally taught kids procedural display. Kids get very good at sensing what the real curriculum is in school and giving it back to us.

When Bloome did some informal research for *The Report Card on Basal Readers,*[1] interviewing kids about basal readers, the kids knew what the curriculum was. The curriculum wasn't the stories. They told us the stories were unimportant. What was important? What was the real curriculum? The stories were there for you to practice the words and the skills. Those were important. And how did they know those were important? Because that's what they got tested on, and obviously the stories didn't really matter. The wholes were for practice, but reading was a part-language curriculum.

Now, of course, the fact that the stories aren't very interesting or aren't much like real language doesn't help either. Even by the time that the kids get to the purged, edited, and censored children's literature of later levels of basals, it still is not the central focus of the program.

We have people now that are turning supposed literature or literature-based programs into the same kind of part-language curriculum. These programs provide worksheets for *Charlotte's Web*[2] so that kids can go through and pick out all the words that start with B or S. Or they can find all the words that rhyme with spider. You can turn whole language into parts by treating it as part-language. Then again, the message is that skills and words, not the joy and knowledge of the book, are what really matters. The part-language curriculum is imposed on the literature experiences through this basalization, through the use of part-language standardized tests, and through focusing the children away from meaningful wholes and toward isolated bits and pieces.

BUILDING CURRICULUM SENSIBLY

Now I want to give an example of how one goes about building a curriculum sensibly. In New Zealand a few years ago they decided it was time to take a new look, nationally, at the school curriculum. They got a lot of people together from all walks of life, not leaving the educators out as we tend to do. In the United States, President Bush had a summit conference on education and did not have a single teacher there. That's the level at which teachers are regarded, and it will continue to happen until teachers demand the right to be heard about curriculum, methodology, and school organization.

What Roger Farr calls the Toyota report, *A Nation at Risk,*[3] blames the schools because Toyotas are selling better than American cars. I've got news for the committee: A lot of the people that design those Toyotas were educated in the United States, and some ideas from here have gotten more attention there than they have here for a variety of reasons that have nothing to do with schools.

In New Zealand they developed a broad consensus on what it was that kids ought to learn. And then they brought this together and got groups of educators (various administrators, teachers, and so forth) together with community people again to move this along and flesh it out into a preliminary national curriculum policy. Next, this got translated into the kind of implementation documents that, at the local level, school by school, could be turned into operational curriculum.

They understand something that we have still had a hard time learning but whole language teachers are helping people to understand: The real curriculum is designed in the transactions between the kids and the teachers in the classroom. Within the broad national curriculum policies and objectives, the actual curriculum emerges within the reality of a particular group of kids from a particular background in a particular neighborhood. That means that the curriculum is built at all levels, with many people having the opportunity to contribute to it, but it is never somebody else's curriculum; it's always particularized in each community, school, and curriculum. And that's a process that doesn't stop. It keeps working all the time.

Now you can argue that New Zealand is a smaller country, three million people. It also happens to be one of the most literate countries in the world, with one of the most sensible educational systems. Imagine a country where kids start school on the Monday closest to their fifth birthday whenever it falls during the year. It's too sensible for us to do that. I have two grandsons, one born September 6 and the other November 28, but because the one that was born November 28 lives in Los Angeles, he'll start school in the September before he's five. That's because the cutoff date is December 1 in California. But the one who lives in Tucson will be six days too late to start school the September before he's five, so he'll wait another year. It's not a very sensible way of doing things.

ONE-LEGGED MODELS

Now sensibility has to do with logic, with reason, with science, that is, with using the best information. We don't have that. What we have are tradition-encrusted part-language curricula. We have another kind of thing, and it isn't exclusive to North America, but we kind of specialize in this. It's what I call "one-legged models of curriculum." In my little book, *What's Whole in Whole Language,*[4] I talk about four pillars of whole language: learning, teaching, language, curriculum. I added the fifth, the social pillar, while traveling in Australia because they helped me to be aware of the fact that we have to remember that the classroom is a social community, that it exists within a society, and that learning is always both personal and social.

One-legged models rest on only one pillar often very narrowly construed. Take for example Madeline Hunter. She has an article called "Madeline Hunter in the English Classroom" in the *English Journal.*[5] She's built on a single psychological leg her view of learning, which goes back to Thorndike as his learning theory has been developed by behavioral psychologists.

She can't understand when whole language teachers tell her and their administrators that whole language and Madeline Hunter simply aren't compatible because, she says, "But I'm only saying that teachers should think." She's not saying they should think; she's telling them how to think, and that's a profound difference. She's telling them to think in terms of the categories of behavioral psychology where everything is geared to a view of conditioned response in a mediational dressing.

Let me give you her ideas for the English curriculum as she suggests them in her article. She has selected a set of quite disparate instructional objectives; she doesn't attempt to connect these or to indicate where they would come from. And that's one of the problems of this kind of one-legged model. She has one objective, for instance, that students will demonstrate an interest in Shakespeare. Another objective is that students will identify prepositions and use them in sentences. Another objective is that, using a sentence starter, students will collaborate to create sentences that require colons and semicolons. In discussing this objective she uses an example that is wrong by my criteria. Such mistakes are not uncommon in this type of curriculum because they tend toward oversimplifications of the very conventions they are trying to teach and do not reside in any overall view of linguistic function or purpose.

She has another objective that I think she thought was her clincher: The student will develop a persuasive argument. She has all of the steps neatly laid out—develop a point of view, the arguments to support, the arguments against, and so on. Again there is oversimplification building on a narrow one-legged model. In her example, every pupil will show this competence to argue persuasively by persuading the teacher to give less homework. I think she picked a bad topic, because in a school where homework is mandatory, no matter how persuasive the kids are, they'll get homework anyway.

In Hunter's one-legged model the jargon is all from behavioral psychology—terms like *guided practice* and *input practice*. With elementary teachers there is also a lot of snapping fingers and clapping hands to get kids' attention. In certain situations, I probably have used some of the techniques she's talking about too. When I have, however, I've always been aware that if the curriculum were more complete, more interesting, more involving, I wouldn't have to use behavioral manipulation to keep the kids involved.

But I want to know where these objectives come from and how the curriculum is determined. Who decided that it was important for the kids to know Shakespeare at all? I'm not saying that they shouldn't; I'm saying, why should they? And in what context and for what purpose and how does it relate to some kind of overarching goal or objective that's relevant to these particular learners? Who decided that the kids should be able to identify prepositions or that they can't do that already, and how is the instruction related to what we know about language learning? How, in fact, does the instruction relate to how kids learn prepositions?

I have a personal memory. I got to seventh grade and for the first time I was given a standardized test that used the word preposition and I panicked—I thought I'd missed that week in school or something. What I did, in fact, as all good test-takers do, is reason backwards from the test items to infer what they were getting at. It worked, partially.

There's no way you can teach prepositions the way Hunter wants to do it. Her examples give kids sentences and ask which is the preposition here. She's got a jazzy way of doing it that sounds like you connect to experiences of learners because she asks the kid who's bored and staring out the window what kind of car he would like to have. He says a Porsche. She says, "Okay. Jim is driving in his Porsche? What's the preposition?" The fact that we're talking about Porsches doesn't make the preposition any more interesting or obvious. In fact, most book examples confuse prepositions with particles anyway, which is because most teachers are only hazy about what prepositions are when you take them out of context.

Yet I have never met a four-year-old who did not learn to use prepositions correctly. So the curricular question that I must raise is why are we wasting time in high school getting kids to show that they can identify prepositions? The time for using the term *preposition* or *colon* or *semicolon* or dealing with the concepts involved is in the course of real reading and writing when there is purpose, authentic context, and an involvement on the part of the learner that would make the focus on the relationship of part to whole a sensible, purposeful one. In other words, we must look at language, at learning, at social context, at teaching, and at curriculum and not just at a narrow model of learning to have effective experiences for kids.

Another one-legged model with some prestigious people behind it is the mastery-learning model. Mastery learning says that if I teach things sequentially and each thing is learned to mastery then I will be sure that everybody will learn. I keep wondering if they know the old farmer's joke about the boy who figured out he could be the strongest person in the world by lifting a growing calf every day until it was a yearling. He'd lift that calf as it got a little heavier and a little heavier, and by the end of the year he'd be lifting a steer that weighed half a ton. What's wrong with that? Well at some point he is going to put his shoulder under it, and he won't be able to lift it.

Mastery learning is like mastery lifting; it makes the assumption that as long as something is neatly sequenced, it's easy to do. But where does the sequence come from? When a group of scholars, including many behaviorists, were given the task of deciding what were the sequential skills in reading, they couldn't agree and said, in fact, that the research was inconclusive. It's not only inconclusive; it's wrong. There are no sequential skills in reading. Language happens all at once, and you learn how the parts relate to the whole not by learning sequential skills but by trying to make sense of the whole of a written-language text, which is the same way you learned to make sense of oral language.

One of the things that mastery learning can't deal with is what kids know before they come to school, because that would require them to pay a lot more attention to kids. The logic of mastery learning requires a curriculum carefully tailored to where each learner is and what already has been learned. But the one-legged model only develops an arbitrary sequence of skills and subskills that are supposed to lead inexorably to mastery. This then is applied invariably to every learner with no concern for who or where the learner is.

Chicago schools tried to have every kid in the same grade on the same page in the mastery-learning sequence at the same point. Every class covered the same material in a given week, and all children in each class proceeded at the same pace. They invented something they were very proud of in Chicago that they added to the mastery learning, called whole class teaching. That simply means everybody's doing the same thing at the same time. When I critiqued the Chicago Mastery Learning-Reading material, I found a workbook page designed to teach number words. There was one item, multiple choice with little pictures, in which children were supposed to pick which picture showed three feet. There were three wrong answers and then a picture showing three disembodied left feet. So when I wrote a critique of it I called it the program with three left feet. [6] What that ignores is that children at very early ages learn that feet come in pairs, one left and one right. They often are aware that animals either have two or four or six or eight feet, but there are no animals that have three feet. That's not the way nature works. And it's going to bother those kids when they get to that item if they know something about feet coming in pairs. Of course some kids will have learned not to let sense get in the way; just figure out what procedure is the right one to display.

When the textbooks become the curriculum, that's another one-legged model. The text series is the curriculum, so it controls the teachers and pupils, and it contains all the necessary experiences for learning to take place. Because this textbook model will be the whole curriculum, it must be tightly sequenced according to a narrow view of its purpose and content. In reading that means again going back to linear and hierarchical views of learning and imposing them on language learning and development.

The popular view is that the text series are written by the outstanding experts in the field (or at least some of them). In fact the design and writing of the actual texts are done by a large group of junior editors. Those "experts" listed as authors are likely to do very little writing and serve more as an advisory panel. More recently publishers have sometimes decided not to bother to hire their own editors or staff. They contract with a textbook mill that grinds out materials on subcontracts. It's much cheaper that way.

I think of the junior editors sitting in their cubicles at these textbook mills like the monks in the Middle Ages endlessly copying manuscripts with no original input because that might be considered a sin. If you read Umberto Eco's *The Name of the Rose*,[7] you know there were monks in this fourteenth-century monastery that contained all the books in the world who believed that everything that would ever need to be written had already been written.

I just read a report to the Senate Republican Policy Committee [8] that says we should stop spending on research in classrooms; it's only experimentation using kids as guinea pigs. We know what we need to know.

The International Reading Association estimates that more than one thousand research papers are prepared each year on the subject of literacy. For the past 50 years, America's classrooms have been used by psychologists, sociologists, educationists, and politicians as a giant laboratory for unproven, untried theories of learning, resulting in a near collapse of public education. It's time we move away from "what's new" and move toward "what works."

It's hard to understand how unproven, untried new ideas could be proven and tried without classroom research. And blaming illiteracy on reading research is like blaming disease on medical research. Never mind. Like Eco's fourteenth-century monks, the Republican Senate Policy document says knowledge, in itself, is dangerous. That's what I call the modern "know-nothing" movement. "What works" for the writers of that document is good old-fashioned phonics.

Ironically, American teachers and learners have been locked into puerile, sanitized, and uninspired basals on the assumption that they represent the best of current knowledge. In fact, they are commercial products resting solidly on the bottom line of the profit and loss statement. And today's basal publisher is part of a megamedia corporation quite likely owned by a German, British, or Australian mogul.

When the textbook becomes the curriculum, everything else is irrelevant—who the kids are, where they come from, what their backgrounds are, what professional competence the teacher has, what teachers know about what the kids need. The issue becomes coverage, and I know very diligent teachers that work and work and work and can't get through the damn fourth-grade reading program with the black-line ditto masters and the workbook pages.

And then their pupils go into a whole language class, and within a month the kids have read more than they read the whole previous year because now the textbook isn't the curriculum—there's a much richer, broader curriculum. I know of school districts (one is Rockford, Illinois, as of last year) that require so much adherence to the textbook that a teacher has to turn in a report every week on the end-of-level test for that particular week's basal-reader assignment. I know of another district in Vancouver, Washington, that actually says the basal reader is the reading curriculum and teachers and kids will be judged on the basis of progress on the tests. Mesa, Arizona, has also warned its teachers that they must teach directly from the basal every day and use the basal tests in making virtually all instructional decisions.

The tests in the basals, I can tell you from our research, are the worst tests of all. They are neither norm-referenced nor criterion-referenced. And more decisions are made about kids' lives in the United States on the basis of end-of-level scores on reading tests than even standardized tests. Kids are failed or passed on the basis of basal tests.

The other side of that is when you make the tests the curriculum and then you go the next step, making the test the judge of merit pay or anything else, what happens is you get cheating. It's been in the literature for years. When the tests are supreme, everybody cheats. The kids cheat, the teachers cheat, the parents cheat, the adminstrators cheat; that's because the issues of learning have been forgotten and the only important thing is gain scores on tests.

PHONICS, THE PHAR RIGHT, CONGRESS, AND THE CENTER FOR THE STUDY OF READING

The far right is trying to force on teachers the ultimate one-legged model. And they're doing it through Congress, the U.S. Department of Education, and the Center for the Study of Reading, which has allowed itself to be co-opted for the purpose. The beginning was through lobbying Congress to require the Department of Education to do a study of research on beginning reading that would prove that programs that use systematic, intensive phonics work best. The Department of Education then ordered the Center for the Study of Reading to do the study. The Center cooperated; they were threatened with loss of all or part of their funds if they didn't. They contracted with Marilyn Adams to write a book that subsequently was published by MIT Press. [9] It's a weighty tome priced at almost $30. The Center then commissioned staff members to produce a 150-page summary of the original book to be distributed widely at a subsidized price of $5.[10]

The report purports, once again, to end the phonics-whole word controversy once and for all by offering still another one-legged view of reading, this time limited to research done by experimental psychologists. Ironically, the focus of the far right was intensive, systematic phonics. Adams's report winds up as a polemic for reading as a process of recognizing words with phonics as the major beginning instructional strategy. Adams's research summary was limited almost exclusively to studies that focused on words as their language unit, so it's not surprising that she reached such a conclusion. She presents a model of reading that is centered on recognition of words in order, which is strangely at odds with the schema-theory view of Richard Anderson and most of his colleagues at the Center.

CURRICULUM AT THE CHALK FACE

All of these one-legged models miss the essence of whole language curriculum and don't understand what our more sensible friends in New Zealand have known all along. To build successful programs for all kids, we have to use the full range of knowledge available in a holistic and integrated way.

I want you to know though that those of us in whole language who are arguing that curriculum has to be whole, has to be complete, has to be rich, has to include all the genres, has to involve kids in using language, not simply learning about it, are referred to in the Blumenfeld newsletter as Ken Goodman's English-as-Chinese Groupies.

Meanwhile Ken Goodman's English-as-Chinese groupies began developing their whole-language approach. As the movement spread throughout the profession, the proponents of phonics were alerted to its dangers. They were the only people in the profession who might prevent the whole language movement from getting off the ground.[11]

Blumenfeld found a quotation from me criticizing an article reporting that a linguist and psychologist taught black inner-city kids in Philadelphia some Chinese ideographs and were surprised that they could learn them with meanings attached. In my critique, I said I didn't think that was surprising: Little Chinese kids have been learning those characters for years.[12] Blumenfeld wants to simplify the world: If you don't support systematic, intensive phonics as a complete method of reading instruction, you must be against the alphabet and for teaching kids to read English like it was written with Chinese characters. In the process he appeals to ethnic and racial feelings of his audience: He implies that our alphabetic writing is superior to anything the Chinese produced.

There are lots of people in the world today who don't read with alphabetic systems, and we need to get our ethnocentricities straight. Alphabetic writing serves us well. But lots of people read very well, and have so for many centuries, without it. That's because the reading process is essentially built around trying to make sense of written language. Virtually the whole world uses a common ideographic writing system for mathematics and finance. "1 + 1 = 2" does not represent the sounds of any one language. Each symbol represents a concept, an idea. And people without a word of language in common can understand this representation of a mathematical statement equally well. That's a big advantage.

I've got news for Mr. Blumenfeld. As flattered as I am by his suggestion that the entire whole language movement is composed of my groupies, I firmly believe that there would be a whole language movement if there had never been a Ken Goodman. That's because today's teachers have the professional know-how and have found their voices. I'm delighted that in the process of creating whole language, these teachers have found value in my work. But they would have done what they've done anyway. He knows that too. All of us are his targets.

Never have American professors and teachers of reading acted more irresponsibly in the face of a serious national problem of growing illiteracy. If it were in our power to do so, we'd fire the lot of them tomorrow.

In England now, the conservative government under Maggie Thatcher decided that they needed a national curriculum, and that caused, when we were there a couple of years ago, some serious worry among the educators. But, so far, it's turned out to be fine. The public, the people involved, the professional educators have built an essentially holistic, comprehensive curriculum that takes into account things like language and multicultural differences. The teachers in England refused to be left out of the process of curriculum making. They insisted that their expertise be recognized. And what emerged is a strong, sound, and positive document, which will be good for the young people of England.

Now they are worried about the evaluation of the curriculum. Teams are at work all over England developing appropriate assessments. Again I have great confidence that what emerges will be progressive and forward looking. The Centre for Language in Primary Education has already developed *The Primary Language Record*, [13] an interview-based assessment, which is a marvelous alternative to the kind of standardized testing we do.

There are a lot of more respectable people in education than Samuel Blumenfeld who have misunderstood the nature of the whole language movement because they don't respect and trust teachers. So they give credit for the grass-roots movements to gurus and miss the dynamic nature of the movement, its roots in history and in solid theory and research, and the explosion of ideas coming from classrooms.

The real place where curriculum happens is what the British call the chalk face. Their metaphor, when they want to talk about the real world, is the coal face, where the miner is down in the coal mine facing that coal seam. Well, we as teachers know exactly what that means. It's hard work being at the chalk face with the real kids in the real classroom. With thirty to thirty-five kids with lots of different needs, it's not easy to do a real curriculum even with the support of school administrators. And in the United States, often there is no such support.

But we do what Dewey told us a long time ago.[14] We start where the learners are. The essentials of this whole language curriculum being formed at the chalk face have been well understood for decades. What we bring to the process that was not available before is a lot more scientific knowledge in the heads of teachers. Teachers know a lot more about how to use the wonderful range of available materials to build on the remarkable strengths of kids. We know these things as a profession, and we know them as individual teachers in our own classrooms.

Dewey told us to start where the learner is. We now understand that developing control of reading and writing begins well before kids start school. Research on early print awareness and emergent literacy that has been done all over the world has shown that kids growing up in literate environments come to school with a strong base to build upon. Teachers know that kids don't come to school as blank slates. Emilia Ferriero [15] asks why we would expect kids to pay attention to everything in the world and then to ignore the print in the environment.

In whole language classrooms, we accept Dewey's notion of learning by doing. We appreciate that children, before they come to school, have already been learning by doing outside of school, and, wow, do they know a lot. So we don't ignore what they already know; we build on it. The whole language literacy curriculum makes connections. We know what to expect in learners, and we know how to find where they are in their development.

In Wendy Hood's bilingual classroom in Tucson, Arizona, the first thing on the first day of school that happens as her kindergartners arrive is that there's a sheet for the kids that says "Sign in, please. Firme aqui."[16] She and her aide greet the kids either in Spanish or English, and the kids sign their names.

That helps her to know where they are; she watches them and learns which kids can sign their names legibly, which kids have some of the letters right and which kids at the end are still standing there with tears in their eyes not quite understanding what they were asked to do. And that's where she begins; her curriculum starts there.

CONTENT AND LEARNER

The whole language curriculum unites the learner with the content. Dewey said, in defining the curriculum, that two points determine the curriculum—the learner and the content—just as two points determine a straight line. Whole language teachers like Wendy understand where learners are; the teachers are professional kid-watchers who use what they learn in their careful observations to build on what kids know and can do.

In Debra Goodman's fifth-grade inner-city classroom, where she has a wide multicultural range, they do a roots unit; each kid does an oral history. They interview parents and grandparents, they talk to their aunts and uncles, they inquire into where they came from, and they learn a lot about themselves. But they also locate themselves in American history. History isn't something that happened to other people. One girl found out that her great-grandfather moved from Quebec to Michigan because the trees were all chopped down in Quebec and so they moved on to chop down the trees in Michigan. And she also learned that her family's New Year's Eve is a French-Canadian celebration and that their Christmas dinner is really an Italian tradition from her maternal grandparents.

Black kids discover how their families came up, like Mildred Taylor's family's moving from the South to the North during World War II because there were jobs there and how they were involved in civil rights. [17] When a black grandmother tells a grandson of her own personal trials and suffering, that child has a sense of himself in relation to history.

MATERIALS IN A WHOLE LANGUAGE CURRICULUM

In this way of studying history a whole language classroom would need some materials; students might even use some textbooks if they have relevant information. But the inquiries of the kids, not the textbooks, drive the curriculum.

What a remarkable revolutionary decision the California Curriculum Commission made when it said that instead of simply choosing from what publishers offered it would take its own state curriculum documents like the English language-arts framework, which now includes reading, and use the criteria in these as specifications for instructional materials. Only materials that fit the California criteria would be considered.

California didn't make an adoption in spelling last year. Nothing offered fit its criteria. Canadian school districts have been doing this sort of material selection for years. Isn't this the way it should be? Why should we have to choose from what publishers offer us? How else are we going to get the publishers to give us better materials?

This year, at the business meeting, NCTE passed a resolution that said that whenever materials are adopted, first of all teachers should be part of the decision making, and second, teachers should always have the option of choosing not to use those materials. As professionals, teachers have the right not to choose those materials! They have the right to choose alternatives. It's not much power, as Bess Altwerger says, if all the power a teacher has is to use this basal or that basal or to use it one way or another way. That's not what we need. We need to put the materials as resources in the hands of the teachers, not make the teacher a resource for delivering the materials.

THE DUAL CURRICULUM

The whole language curriculum is a dual curriculum. Halliday, a linguist, has taught us an important lesson about language learning: At the same time you learn language, you learn through language because the reason you're learning language is as a way of communicating with other people.

Halliday calls his study of his son learning language *Learning How to Mean.* [18] Language learning is also learning how to mean things the way people mean them to each other. Babies come to understand what people say to them, and they learn to make themselves understood to others. And Halliday also says that in the process of learning language and learning through language, you also learn about language. Everybody has experienced a four-year-old who says what does so and so mean, picking up a word that he or she has heard. Some people want to call that metalinguistic; I think it's simply that kids become aware of language and are interested in it in the course of using it and learning through it.

My grandson Aaron is an expert on dinosaurs, as many kids are these days. When he was about five he was in a drugstore that had a display of little plastic dinosaurs. Aaron went up to the clerk and said, "What's the name of this dinosaur?" And she said, "You can call it anything you want when you get home, dear." He wanted to know its scientific name.

CURRICULUM FOR ALL LEARNERS: RESPECTING DIFFERENCE

We need to understand and we are understanding the importance of looking at similarities between learners, understanding how learning in general develops and at the same time accepting and appreciating difference: the difference that comes from culture, the difference that comes from language, or the difference that comes simply from being interested in different things.

I love literature, but that doesn't mean that a kid is illiterate unless he reads novels. Some kids prefer to read nonfiction; some prefer to read how-to-do-it kinds of things. Yes, we want to broaden kids' interest. But more important is to build on who they are, what they are, on their self-appreciation. And one of the things we understand is that no curriculum can be successful that doesn't accept learners at the point where they are when they come to us. We don't have the right to force learners to change anyway.

Dewey said it again for us. Schools can choose between two alternatives: to make learners adjust to the school or to adjust the school to the learners. If the schools have a fixed curriculum built around tests and textbooks, there's no way to adjust it to the learner. If there is, on the other hand, a situation where the school is going to adjust to the learner, then that requires the understanding that different kids require different things and that choice is a terribly important part of learning. Learners must have the right to choose what to write about, what to read, and the purposes for doing things.

The dual whole language curriculum builds language and thinking in the course of building knowledge and schema and ways of solving problems. Those are inseparable objectives. People who are talking about higher-order thinking skills are off the mark. First of all I want to know what about the lower-order and middle-order thinking skills. Most of the things they describe as higher-order thinking skills, we find happening at all levels when we analyze reading. If you have to draw inferences about what the next letter is, what the meaning of a sentence is, whether this is going to be a question or statement, those inferences require the same kind of thinking strategies that happen when we're talking about figuring out who done it in a murder mystery or trying to solve some human problems. We learn to think to use language in the course of real speech acts and literary events. The dual whole language curriculum builds thought and language as it builds knowledge.

The dual curriculum puts an interesting twist on what's happening in classrooms because very often the teacher is watching the kids—as a kid watcher—in terms of language and thinking development while the kids think; what they are basically doing is solving problems, answering questions, finding out the things that they need to know.

Once in a while the focus for the learners also shifts to language itself. They begin to look at language: Isn't this way of saying that interesting; how do we do this in English (or Spanish); and how does language work, anyhow? One of the things we know about development is that most of the time the less attention you pay to language and to thinking, the better they develop as long as you're using them in authentic contexts.

ALL LANGUAGE GENRES

In a whole language curriculum we expand our focus to get the kids into using different kinds of genres: writing letters because there's a need for real correspondence, not because it's the next thing in the English book; learning how to do a report when it's appropriate, not because doing a report is a class requirement. There's nothing wrong with report writing being part of the curriculum, but the best way to learn to write a report is when you've got something to report, and that has to be as part of an investigation, a study, a development of information that's part of asking questions and seeking knowledge. In that context kids will build a schema for the report genre and not be satisfied with the report being two paragraphs copied from an encyclopedia.

In Debra's roots unit, the report may be a videotape where the kid is accompanying the videotape with grandparents and other relatives talking about family history while the pupil is using index cards to give an oral presentation. Or it might be an elaborate family tree with an accompanying discussion to help kids read the family tree.

FITTING THE CURRICULUM TO THE LEARNERS

The whole language classroom curriculum recognizes that there are some national concerns and broad cultural objectives for all children in a culture and country. It recognizes that there are state priorities and community concerns that must be included in the curriculum. But those objectives need to be more global as you go up and more particular as you go down so that ultimately the curriculum director for each classroom is the teacher. The teacher is the curriculum director in continuous transactions with the kids: From these transactions the real curriculum emerges.

Bess Altwerger talks, in this book, about activities. Activities may look very much the same in very different programs. The behaviorists taught us a bad lesson, since they didn't believe that you could get into the black box, which was their funny term for the head. So they wanted to look only at stimulus and response. They taught us to frame objectives behaviorally, which often meant that we were focusing on what the kids were doing, the activity, without any underlying reason for the activity.

Madeline Hunter wants those kids to identify the prepositions in sentences at a specified level of accuracy: I want to know why should they do that? What does it relate to?

An activity is never an objective. Its significance comes from its purpose as it relates to a study, which may have an objective like building a sense of yourself in history, which leads to a roots unit, which then leads kids to giving reports in various kinds of media and forms, which then leads to kids questioning each other.

In Debra's class, when the kids report, there are questions about the substantive material, but there are also questions like, What made you think of that way of doing that? Where did you get that idea? How did you get that kind of information? This happens because the kids are involved in process as well as in product because they think of themselves as inquirers, as researchers, as problem solvers.

AUTHENTIC GOALS AND OBJECTIVES

The goals of the whole language curriculum are multiple and interrelated. Yes, there are cognitive goals. We want the kids to have knowledge. We don't need E. D. Hirsch to determine what knowledge we must have. I think he's got a peculiar idea of what people need to know, and what he seems not to have understood is that much of what we teach in school, kids have diligently forgotten over all these years.

I'd like to see a good study of why some things are easily forgotten while other things are so well remembered. From a whole language perspective, I believe that such a study would show that kids remember easily what is functional, interesting, and relevant, and they forget easily what is only learned for the purposes of school. Many years ago a study in Scotland showed that pupils who had passed a grammar test at 11 couldn't pass it when they were 16. In the whole language curriculum, experiences are authentic, so more is learned and more is remembered.

There are also thinking- and learning-strategy objectives. We build strategies for problem solving and for learning from experiences. But then there are effective goals too; how do kids view themselves? How do kids view themselves as individuals, as members of ethnic groups, as members of communities, as speakers of languages and dialects?

Those goals are as important as any other. They are part of the whole of whole language. In the barren, one-legged, "good teacher" model, we can get learners who regurgitate isolated facts and reproduce specific "behaviors" but who don't have a sense of how to shape their values, how to make judgments, how to look at their own moral decisions as they make them.

And in the whole language curriculum, our social goals are also important. John Goodlad in *A Place Called School* [19] reported that in junior high schools the single most important thing to young adolescents that they interviewed was friendship. These young people are tremendously concerned with how they fit in and how others see them. Being accepted and socially at ease may literally be more important than life itself.

We need to create classrooms where kids can make friends, where they can feel at home, where they can feel a part of a social community. When we plan for pupils to work together on thematic units, on problem solving and on writing, we are as concerned for these social objectives as we are for any cognitive ones.

Our democratic society requires citizens to know how to appreciate the needs and rights of others and how to pursue their own interests without hurting other people. The periodic class meeting is not just an extra; it is part of the curriculum. Offering pupils a forum for raising social problems is a serious part of the classroom experience and shows that the teacher treats the social concerns of pupils with respect and proper concern.

Whole language classrooms are run democratically to build the vital ability to participate in a democracy. Kids learn to work together, to plan together, and to be accepting of others. We build a sense of community and of mutual support. In many whole language classrooms the kids understand that they will have a choice of which classmates they work with but at some time during the year everyone will work with everyone else. Many whole language teachers have built on the value that if you have knowledge or ability, you must be willing to share them with others, you must be willing to offer help and support when it is asked for. An important social objective in whole language classrooms is learning to care for each other.

Our whole language concepts of teaching and curriculum need to be expanding. They need, as Bess Altwerger has said, to be empowering in the sense of the word as she's using it, and they need to be liberating. We can't liberate kids from the real world. We can help them to deal with it, and that may help them to liberate themselves. We can't liberate them from the laws of physics or from economic circumstances or from political realities, but we can surely liberate them from textbooks. We can liberate them from tests. We can liberate them from the arbitrary floors and ceilings that graded arbitrary curriculum puts on them. And we can provide a curriculum that then liberates them to use the energies and the talents and the powers that they have.

There's so much more in the world for kids to learn than the traditional, part-language, and one-legged curricula have offered. We want it all in the whole language curriculum.

NOTES

1. Goodman, K. P. Shannon, Y. Freeman, and S. Murphy. *Report Card on Basal Readers.* Katonah, New York: Richard C. Owen, 1988.

2. White, E. B. *Charlotte's Web.* New York: Dell, 1952.

3. National Commission on Excellence in Education. *A Nation at Risk.* Washington, D.C.: U.S. Government Printing Office, 1983.

4. Goodman, K. *What's Whole in Whole Language.* Portsmouth, New Hampshire: Heinemann, 1986.

5. Goodman, K. "Commentary: Chicago Mastery Learning Reading: A Program with 3 Left Feet," *Education Week,* p. 20, October 9, 1985

6. Hunter, Madeline "Madeline Hunter in the English Classroom," *English Journal,* September 1989.

7. Eco, Umberto. *The Name of the Rose.* New York: Harcourt, Brace, Jovanovich, 1983.

8. U.S. Senate Republican Policy Committee "Illiteracy: An Incurable Disease or Education Malpractice," unpublished paper, September 13, 1989.

9. Adams, M. "Beginning to Read: Thinking and Learning about Print: A Summary." Prepared by S. Stahl, J. Osborne, and F. Lehr. Urbana: Center for the Study of Reading, 1990.

10. Adams, M. *Beginning to Read: Thinking and Learning About Print.* Cambridge, Massachusetts: MIT Press, 1990.

11. *The Blumenfeld Education Letter,* p. 6, March 1989.

12. Goodman, K. "The 13th Easy Way to Make Learning to Read Difficult," A Reaction to Gleitman and Rozin. *Reading Research Quarterly,* VIII:4., Summer 1973.

13. Barrs, M., S. Ellis, H. Hester, and A. Thomas. *Primary Language Record.* London: Inner London Education Authority, Centre for Language and Primary Education, 1989.

14. Archambault, R.D. (Ed.) *John Dewey on Education.* Chicago, Illinois: University of Chicago Press, 1964.

15. Ferreiro, E. and Teberosky, A. *Literacy Before Schooling.* Portsmouth, New Hampshire: Heinemann, 1982.

16. Hood, W. "If the Teacher Comes Over Pretend It's a Telescope?" in Goodman, K., Goodman, Y., and Hood, W. (Eds) *The Whole Language Evaluation Book.* Portsmouth. New Hampshire: Heinemann, 1989.

17. Taylor, M. *Let the Circle Be Unbroken.* New York: Bantam, 1981.

18. Halliday, M. A. K. *Learning How to Mean.* London: Edward Arnold, 1975.

19. Goodlad, J. *A Place Called School.* New York: McGraw-Hill, 1984.

Kenneth S. Goodman is a professor of education at the University of Arizona. His recent efforts include developing a teacher-education course that teaches whole language and is whole language.

CAROLE EDELSKY

Critique

A CRITICAL COMPONENT IN CONTENT STUDY

This panel on problems and possibilities at the chalk face is bifurcated: Some of us are to present problems; others are to present future possibilities. I've been asked to present problems—problems in the way content (social studies and science) is handled currently in many whole language classrooms. The assignment to be critical of the content study going on in the name of whole language is a difficult one for two reasons. First, it is ripe with potential for creating bad feelings in both the audience and the speaker (that is, me). An audience reads or listens and can't help wondering if they too are included in the criticism. And for my part as presenter, I can't help noticing the cool response I get to thoughtful criticism in contrast to the warm response I receive when I offer inspirational or future-oriented messages. Second, this is also a hard task because even though we say whole language is about education in general—that it's not just a way to teach reading—there is actually not as much emphasis in published materials or in conference presentations on the study of content in a whole language classroom as there is on literacy, so I won't have such a widely shared set of ideas to build on (see Newman, 1985, for an exception).

Even though it may be hard to criticize the way content is being offered in many whole language classrooms, the critique is necessary. Whole language is about education in general. It's about curriculum, instruction, classroom interaction, evaluation, school-community relations, teachers' professional growth—everything connected with school and with learning. And it has a coherent, principled theoretical basis that is relevant to education in general. That is, whole language is a coherent overarching *perspective.* But whole language is also a *movement.* And as a movement, it is being both co-opted and misrepresented, with its name applied to everything and anything. It is being co-opted by those who want to cash in on its popularity—e.g., by publishers selling whole language basals, or by consultants who gave workshops on reading skills last week but who are now offering workshops on so-called whole language reading skills this week. And it is being misrepresented by both its enemies (who say whole language has no consistent definition) and by some of its friends (who say the same thing in another way—that, because whole language respects the multiplicity of interpretations, it means whatever anyone says it means).

Whole language is *not* whatever anybody says it is. After years of hearing people misrepresenting her presentation of the theory of reading as a transactional process, Louise Rosenblatt (1985) finally had to perform what she called a "terminological rescue operation" to try to undo misconceptions. Whole language may need the same treatment. Before it became a movement, whole language was a *perspective,* and it still is—a perspective on language and language acquisition. Whole language people take principles from that perspective and extend them to more than just the learning of oral or written language. They find in these principles a guide for, as I said, everything connected with school, including the study of content.

People who sincerely (not just opportunistically, like many publishers) see themselves as part of whole language as a movement have an obligation to come to deeply understand whole language as a *perspective*, to learn how and why it isn't just an attractive set of activities to do that makes kids and teachers feel better about school. Right now, the term *whole language* opens a lot of doors (it closes some too, but for now it mostly opens them). It's a new, popular, desirable label. In other words, whole language as a movement makes the climate more hospitable both for those who already hold whole language beliefs and for those who want to learn those beliefs—and we're thankful for that. But as the label is used more and more indiscriminately, skeptics will be able to say, "See, it doesn't work" (and, of course, if things keep on progressing as they are, they will be right, since "it" wasn't whole language in the first place). And that will make it harder for people who do have a truly whole language *perspective.* Not that they'll revert to their pre-whole language thinking. But they'll have to go underground again or else they'll have to battle *constantly* (instead of just intermittently, which is what I meant before by a "hospitable climate") for the space to provide what is best for children. Such battles may provide grist for great teacher war stories, but they make daily life as a true whole language teacher very hard. And, of course, the energy put into those battles is subtracted from the energy necessary for giving children the best education possible.

We need to begin to differentiate between what is congruent with a whole language *perspective* on language and language learning and what is not, and we need to be able to *say* what language and learning principles we're invoking when we make those distinctions. Let me try to do that a bit for content studies—the learning and teaching of science and social studies in particular. I'll point out just two of the many whole language principles that seem to be missing from much of the science and social studies that are being called whole language.

SOME WHOLE LANGUAGE PRINCIPLES

Principle 1. In the relation between content and skills or tools, skills or tools are secondary—they *serve* content.

Principle 2. People learn by doing. We learn to use language by using language, we learn science by doing science, history by doing history—that is, there's a key whole language principle that says we learn and teach through actual use or actual doing of whatever it is, not through exercises or practice so we can *do it* later.

Principle 1: Skills or Tools Serve Content

If a teacher believes that symbolic skills and tools (speech, reading, mapping, and so on) serve content, that means she's not thinking up topics to study (like dinosaurs or bears or magnets) in order to make the skills more interesting or in order to integrate the teaching of subjects like art (pictures of dinosaurs), math (doing story problems on dinosaurs), geography (locating where dinosaur remains have been found), and spelling and writing (using dinosaur words in stories). Instead, the children in that teacher's class are studying *dinosaurs*, trying to answer live questions they have about dinosaurs. If they need to use maps to answer some of their questions, that's when the whole language teacher shows them how to use maps. If they don't need maps, the children learn map reading or mapmaking some time when they *do* need it.

Whatever skills and tools and subjects are needed are used in order to study dinosaurs—how they lived or died or what arguments people have had about dinosaurs and who won those arguments, and how they may not be won for all time, and how those scientific victories about knowledge are or have been related to other arguments in the society (like the argument over divine or natural origins) and who benefits from the outcomes of those scientific arguments (yes, certain sectors of society benefit directly or indirectly from scientific arguments—even arguments about dinosaurs). Whatever the questions, whatever the direction the study takes, the language skills, the math skills, the scientific skills, and so on are used for interrogating the content. The content—the topic or theme of dinosaurs—is not just glue for making subject-matter fragments stick together.

What's more, if even a quite conventional school topic like dinosaurs can be treated seriously, going beyond the surface to account for the political nature of knowledge, for instance, then it follows that it is not the topic itself that determines whether the curriculum will be one of critique, one that might count in the world. As Bess Altwerger urged this morning (see Altwerger, this volume), the topic can be significant. That is, it can self-consciously aim for critical literacy. It can, for example, be a topic concerning the mundane signs of endemic racism or of gender, ethnic, and class injustice. Or it can be a topic discovered by finding out what is really on kids' minds (Harste, 1989). Often, that is not dinosaurs. Sometimes it's something like nuclear war or parents being out of work or moral issues like what is fair (on the playground or in South Africa or El Salvador). But I want to emphasize here that to be significant content, to be content that contributes to critical literacy, it doesn't mean the topic has to be overtly political; nor does it mean that the topic has to be overtly about conditions of kids' lives or of their immediate neighborhoods. All knowledge is socially constructed. Therefore, all content, all knowing, is political. It is all related somehow to different power positions in society.

Judy Buchanen, a wonderfully sensitive teacher in Philadelphia, gave me a marvelous example of the political nature of knowledge from math, showing the political meaning of those seemingly neutral things called numbers—the sociopolitics of arithmetic, if you will. While talking with her fourth-grade class about recent events around the Berlin Wall, she asked the children if half a million sounded like a bigger number than five hundred thousand. They said yes. She said it did to her too, and isn't it interesting how the papers report the East German border crossings using the number one-half million but they report attendance at certain marches and demonstrations using the number five hundred thousand.

A content study that is congruent with whole language principles—like the principle that skills serve content (and not the other way around)—won't consist of a collection of clever activities all topically related to dinosaurs or spiders or bears or nuclear war. And it can't be *all planned by the teacher at the start of the unit*. Instead, it will take shape as it develops, with one learning experience growing out of the other, in the course of pursuing *a line of inquiry* that develops as the children get more and more involved with their topic. There won't be learning centers or tasks set up to motivate or *engender* interests. But there *would* be centers or tasks devised by teachers *and* children to *satisfy* interests, to help kids *answer* questions that arise as they pursue a topic (Altwerger & Flores, in press). That means that the teacher and children together are negotiating the content and the work. If skills serve content and if content takes its shape from children's interests as they develop over a unit of study, then those canned units or themes that are circulating in some districts just don't fit. As prepackaged units, they put the skills cart before the content horse. They deprive the children of the chance to do the important question formulating, the important brainstorming about resources, the important *thinking*.

If we seriously understand that skills serve content, that tools are used to investigate interests and *not* that interests are opportunistically used for teaching skills, then we would not exploit music and art and literature for nonmusical, nonartistic, nonliterary ends. Music, art, and literature would appear instead for their own sakes. They wouldn't just be ways to augment a science theme. For example, we would not find cases where all the literature is geared to the social studies topic, where the only chance a child has to read *My Brother Sam Is Dead* is if the class happens to be studying the American Revolution, or conversely, where *all* the literature choices during the study of Native Americans are books about Native Americans. *Annie and the Old One* is valuable in its own right; it doesn't need to be granted legitimacy in the curriculum by fitting in with the social studies topic. Music, paintings, sculpture, dance, drama—these can and should stand on their own in classrooms, or at least be used for what they are—aesthetic creations created under particular social, political, and economic conditions. When Chris Boyd's kindergarten class studied Italy, they also studied Da Vinci paintings. But they were looking at the paintings as *paintings*. When, on the other hand, kids are asked to use the Mona Lisa as the game board, to see who can find the most triangles or circles embedded in it, that reveals the *non*-whole language belief that the main point of school is to teach skills like identifying triangles, not to help develop educated people who can view the Mona Lisa with an informed eye.

Principle 2: People Learn by Doing

They learn to read by reading, to write by writing; they learn science and social studies by *doing* science and social studies, which includes *reflecting* on their doing. A simple idea—yet it is being violated over and over again in classrooms designated as "whole language."

In learning to read or write, the difference between really using language and just doing reading or writing exercises has a lot to do with the readers' or writers' purpose. It's the same with science and social studies. Children can do science exercises or they can do what natural and social scientists do. And the difference between the two has to do with *why* they're doing it. For example, in a classroom where whole language principles are not being used (no matter whether the classroom is called a whole language classroom or not), the reason a child might be graphing the distances of various stars from the earth is so she can get a grade or go out for recess or be checked off in a grade book. That is, there is little connection between the child's purpose and the topic of stars. The topic (let's say stars) is in fact irrelevant. As far as that child is concerned, getting checked off is what is important—and she could just as well get checked off for doing a graphing activity about starlings. When there's no connection between the child's purpose and what she's studying, it's a pretty good bet that she's simply engaged in a science exercise, that she's not *doing* science. But where the teacher understands how much the *child's* purpose matters, how one purpose makes something an exercise while another makes it *science*, the teacher tries hard to set things up so that the reason the child is graphing star distances is because she really wants to know about either stars or how far away they are.

In working with the distinction between real use and exercises (or pretend use) and in trying to make sure the curriculum is weighted with real use, with children learning science or social studies by doing what natural and social scientists do, whole language teachers use as their model—what else?—*what natural and social scientists do.* This is one of the critical lessons we've learned from Graves (1983), Calkins (1986), and Atwell (1987). They've taught us to think, what do *writers* do? Kathryn Patterson doesn't use story starters. James Baldwin didn't choose from three topics someone gave him. Anne Tyler doesn't put her hand in a paper bag to feel different textures and write down the texture words. And neither should child writers.

We know that now for writing, so we can see how silly it is. Somehow, we forget the lesson when it comes to natural and social science. But it's the same thing. Astronomers don't spend their time working on hypotheses about astronomical phenomena. Historians don't answer a list of someone else's questions so they can be checked on their knowledge of Civil War facts. *They* check "facts" found by others, and they hunt up new sources as they do their most important work—interpreting what those "facts" mean and what the context was for the sources. Anthropologists don't do clever follow-up activities, like conducting a pretend interview with their favorite informant, when they wind up a study in New Guinea. Whole language teachers know that. It doesn't matter if such follow-up activities are fun and if children like them. They aren't honest science.

Whole language aims for people to become educated. Among other things, that means that they come to really know biological, anthropological, geographical, and historical, to name a few, ways of knowing the world so they can bring those ways of knowing to bear on questions that don't fall neatly within any of these disciplinary boundaries (Edelsky, 1989). The way that happens is by *doing* biology, anthropology, or history as a biologist, anthropologist, or historian would—by being involved in honest scientific endeavor, not by taking part in teacher-planned activities with merely a scientific look.

When people *do* science, they have their own live questions about what *they're* interested in, and they take part in conversations directly or indirectly (live or through books) with other scientists so they can learn what other scientists' questions are and what *they're* doing or have done to answer them. It means figuring out how to formulate questions in ways they can be studied. It means messing with raw data, figuring out how to analyze and make sense of it, making one's own interpretations, anticipating competing interpretations. And teaching children who are *doing* science means provoking new questions and helping them generate insights about questions *they* entertain, not entertaining them with fun activities.

Whole language as a *perspective* has the potential to create educated people who can use their education to struggle, critically, for a better world—but not if whole language as a *movement* just takes the same old unit idea from the 1950s and 1960s, adds a few hands-on activities, contrives ways to tie a science topic in with some art and literature and arithmetic and writing, and calls it by the now-popular name whole language. Whole language is much more than a name, much more than a set of thematically integrated activities. Whole language requires new knowledge—about language and language acquisition. It requires study and reflection about how these insights apply to a total curriculum. It takes individual effort and also collaborative work with other professionals, who are also struggling with the challenges at the chalk face. There just aren't any shortcuts. But here's my ending inspirational note: It's worth it!

REFERENCES

Altwerger, B. and Flores, B. "The Politics of Whole Language." In Goodman, K., Goodman, Y., and Bird, L. B. (Eds.), *The Whole Language Catalogue.* New York: Macmillan-McGraw Hill, (in press).

Atwell, N. *In the Middle.* Upper Montclair, New Jersey: Boynton/Cook, 1987.

Calkins, L. *The Art of Teaching Writing.* Portsmouth, New Hampshire: Heinemann, 1986.

Edelsky, C. "Literacy Education: Reading the Word and the World." *English in Australia,* 89, 62-71, 1989.

Graves, D. *Writing: Teachers and Children at Work.* Exeter, New Hampshire: Heinemann, 1983.

Harste, J. Paper Presented at annual meeting of National Council of Teachers and English, Baltimore, 1989.

Newman, J. *Whole language: Theory in Use.* Portsmouth, New Hampshire: Heinemann, 1985.

Rosenblatt, L. "Transaction Versus Interaction—a Terminological Rescue Operation." *Research in the Teaching of English,* 19, 96-107, 1985.

Carole Edelsky is a faculty member at Arizona State University.

Yetta Goodman

Personal and Social Empowerment

As whole language professionals come together at conferences, workshops, and support groups to talk, our purpose is to help each other consider ideas and to question our own beliefs. My developing beliefs about whole language are honed by my interactions with teachers who share with me what they are doing and challenge what I'm saying. It is from the challenges, the critiques, and the debates at the chalk face that whole language will grow and sustain itself. To highlight that dialogue we must plan for and be seriously involved in continuous scrutiny and intellectual inquiry. We will never agree on all aspects of whole language, but it will be through shared understandings about the nature of our agreements and disagreements that whole language will be nurtured.

When educators and parents come together to explore an idea as dynamic as whole language, the talk that we generate must be translated into activity as we return to our communities and our schools. I would like to explore some suggestions that will encourage whole language advocates— parents or professionals— to take steps toward more personal and social empowerment by echoing Nancie Atwell's words at an NCTE conference.

Nancie talked about the heart and art of teaching and the importance of permitting and encouraging diversity and idiosyncrasy among teachers. She also calls for teachers to be readers and writers, which she says is the most powerful political act of all. I will return to all three of these issues because I see them as basic to personal and social empowerment.

Personal empowerment is best demonstrated by Janine Archey, a third-grade teacher in Royal Oak, Michigan. About a year ago I read a book called *Faithful Elephants* by Yukio Tsuchiya (Houghton Mifflin, 1988) at the Michigan Reading Association in Oakland County. The book retells a story told in Tokyo every year about the last stages of World War II. Tokyo was often being attacked from the air. At the city zoo the keepers were ordered to kill all of the big animals for fear that they would run amok if the zoo were bombed directly. The story describes how three elephants were starved to death at the zoo. I invited teachers to try the book with their kids, knowing that some might find this book controversial. Using controversial ideas is an act of courage and empowerment. Ms. Archey read *Faithful Elephants* to her children because she was interested in getting her kids to think about how everyday conflicts in classrooms can be resolved and how nations resolve conflicts as well. While they were discussing the book, one of the boys said, "You know, I think my grandfather was in that war." The other children also began to remember their grandparents talking about World War II. Ms. Archey asked the students if they would like to write to their grandparents and ask them about their experiences during World War II. The class generated a list of questions and wrote to their grandparents.

Their letters helped them explore issues about World War II, and their grandparents' responses helped them personalize an important time in American history. The grandparents' letters were compiled into a written history about the Second World War. The controversies that surround peace and war issues are explored through the range of personal responses by the grandparents.

Grandparents went into their attics and found many firsthand documents such as ration books and newspaper clippings from around the world and sent them to their grandchildren. There was discussion about women's movement into the workplace as the children read about their grandmothers going off to the factories to support the war effort. One of the grandmothers wrote of how women couldn't wear nylons at that time and described how they painted seams on the back of their legs so they looked as if they were wearing hose. Grandfathers sent the letters they had written home from the fronts. There was a letter written by one grandfather to his little baby whom he had never seen who, of course, was one of the third-graders' fathers.

One letter from Japanese grandparents discusses how they had to decide whether or not to spend the war years in a concentration camp in the western United States or to move to the Midwest. A group of third-graders learned a great deal about an important historical period when Janine Archey was personally empowered to share a controversial book with her children and extend it through an intergenerational unit, which has often been a part of her curriculum.

Nobody can go out and reproduce exactly what Janine Archey did. But Janine Archey has used her art and her heart of teaching to help make connections with the older generation, to discover that history is something each person experiences personally, and to come to grips with issues of peace and war— individual and world conflict. You can't clone a whole language teacher. Teachers need to be willing to discover their personal convictions to share with their students in unique ways.

One of the things that concerns me about the focus in some of the research on teaching today is that it seems to assume that what will emerge from all this study is the model of a single type of effective teacher that all other teachers can then imitate. Personal empowerment comes from knowing ourselves well enough that we are confident to share our personal strengths and abilities with our students.

Our personal empowerment is supported as we become more involved in social empowerment. Let me suggest some specific actions:

In the United States today a national policy that will shape a definition of literacy is developing. The National Assessment of Educational Progress (NAEP) may be used in every state, probably first at fourth grade, to evaluate and compare reading scores. Since tests have such an impact on curriculum, the development of NAEP may establish our nation's definition of literacy. National assessment has been around for some time, but now it is being promoted for everyone to use. As we come together as groups of whole language teachers, we need to respond to issues such as this one. We need to let our congressmen, senators, and state legislators know that we are well informed on this issue and that we can help them think through their positions. We need to ask them how the National Assessment Committee was formed. Why aren't more teachers' and parents' voices being represented by the NAEP? We cannot allow a national policy towards literacy to get going and not be part of the discussion and the debate.

I'm often asked how big the whole language movement is. At no point historically has a reform movement affected more than 10 percent of classrooms. I'm hoping that whole language will be a little different. Although we have never had such a powerful grass-roots movement before, we still are very small in number. Yesterday in one of the meetings, a parent came up to me and said, "I am a parent, I want to educate teachers about whole language." My granddaughter was in a kindergarten and now is in a second grade where the curriculum is rigid and not supportive of what we know about developmentally appropriate learning or language development.

Another possible action for social empowerment is to encourage parents to become part of whole language support movements and to support their efforts. We need parents who are whole language advocates to help other parents understand the advantages of whole language. Many teachers are parents as well. How many of us are yearning for whole language classrooms for our children and grandchildren? We need to form alliances with parents and let them help us spread the word and support our efforts. Through these actions we become advocates for our own children and grandchildren. Our social empowerment comes through our collaboration and actions.

Finally, let me come back to Nancie Atwell's third point. We become personally empowered as we read widely and as we respond to what we read in writing. As we read letters to the editor or editorials about education, let's respond by sharing the views about whole language issues that need wider circulation. When you read something about classrooms and know you've done something unique, write to local newsletters and language-arts or reading journals to share what you are doing and to place the ideas within a whole language philosophical stance. The voices of classroom teachers are being heard and read throughout the land. I urge you all to participate in the opportunities that teachers are taking to explore what they believe and what they know about their students and (as my friend and colleague Dorothy Watson says) "to share their very best" with colleagues and parents through writing.

The real impact of a meeting together is what each of us actively does in response to what we've learned. What are you going to do on Monday at the chalk face?

Yetta Goodman is a professor of education at the University of Arizona. She has worked for years to help teachers listen to children's voices and become kid-watchers.

Perspective From a TAWL Teacher

What will we do indeed? It is a relief to know we are not required to agree—only to examine our beliefs and practices and share our understandings so that when we must lean, it will be on our sense of professionalism and our colleagues'. From this Day of Whole Language, we take away a year of thought and challenge, a strengthening of the garden trellis, and an excitement about facing the challenges at the chalk face.